The Secrets of Ancient Ritual Sites

The Citadel of Machu Picchu and Stonehenge

Ricard Regas and Albert Cañagueral

Cavendish Square

New York

This edition published in 2018 by Cavendish Square Publishing, LLC
243 5th Avenue, Suite 136, New York, NY 10016

First Edition

Cataloging-in-Publication Data

Names: Regas, Ricard. | Cañagueral, Albert.
Title: The secrets of ancient ritual sites / Ricard Regas and Albert Cañagueral.
Description: New York : Cavendish Square Publishing, 2018. | Series: The secrets of history | Includes bibliographical references and index.
Identifiers: ISBN 9781502632746 (library bound) | ISBN 9781502634436 (pbk.)
Subjects: LCSH: Civilization, Ancient--Juvenile literature. | Machu Picchu Site (Peru)--Juvenile literature. | Extinct cities--Juvenile literature. | Stonehenge (England)--Juvenile literature. | Megalithic monuments--England--Wiltshire--Juvenile literature.
Classification: LCC CB311.R44 2018 | DDC 930--dc23

Editorial Director: David McNamara
Editor: Erica Grove
Associate Art Director: Amy Greenan
Production Coordinator: Karol Szymczuk

Original Idea: Sol90 Publishing
Project Management: Nuria Cicero
Editorial Coordination: Diana Malizia
Editorial Team: Alberto Hernández, Virginia Iris Fernández, Mar Valls, Marta de la Serna, Sebastián Romeu. Maximiliano Ludueña, Carlos Bodyadjan, Doris Elsa Bustamante, Tania Domenicucci, Andrea Giacobone, Constanza Guariglia, Joaquín Hidalgo, Hernán López Winne.
Proofreaders: Marta Kordon, Edgardo D'Elio
Design: Fabián Cassan
Layout: Laura Ocampo, Carolina Berdiñas, Clara Miralles, Paola Fornasaro, Mariana Marx, Pablo Alarcón

The photographs in this book are used by permission and through the courtesy of: Corbis Images; Getty Images; National Geographic Stock; Alamy; Scala Archives. Science Photo Library; AGE Fotostock; Lynette Thomas, The Image File; Wiltshire Heritage Museum, Devizes; Adam Stanford of Aerial Cam, (www.aerial-cam.co.uk); Wessex Archaeology (www.wessexarch.co.uk); English Heritage, NMR; © Crown copyright, NMR.

Printed in the United States of America

Metric Conversion Chart

1 inch = 2.54 centimeters; 25.4 millimeters	1 cup = 250 milliliters
1 foot = 30.48 centimeters	1 ounce = 28 grams
1 yard = 0.914 meters	1 fluid ounce = 30 milliliters
1 square foot = 0.093 square meters	1 teaspoon = 5 milliliters
1 square mile = 2.59 square kilometers	1 tablespoon = 15 milliliters
1 ton = 0.907 metric tons	1 quart = 0.946 liters
1 pound = 454 grams	355 degrees Fahrenheit = 180 degrees Celsius
1 mile = 1.609 kilometers	

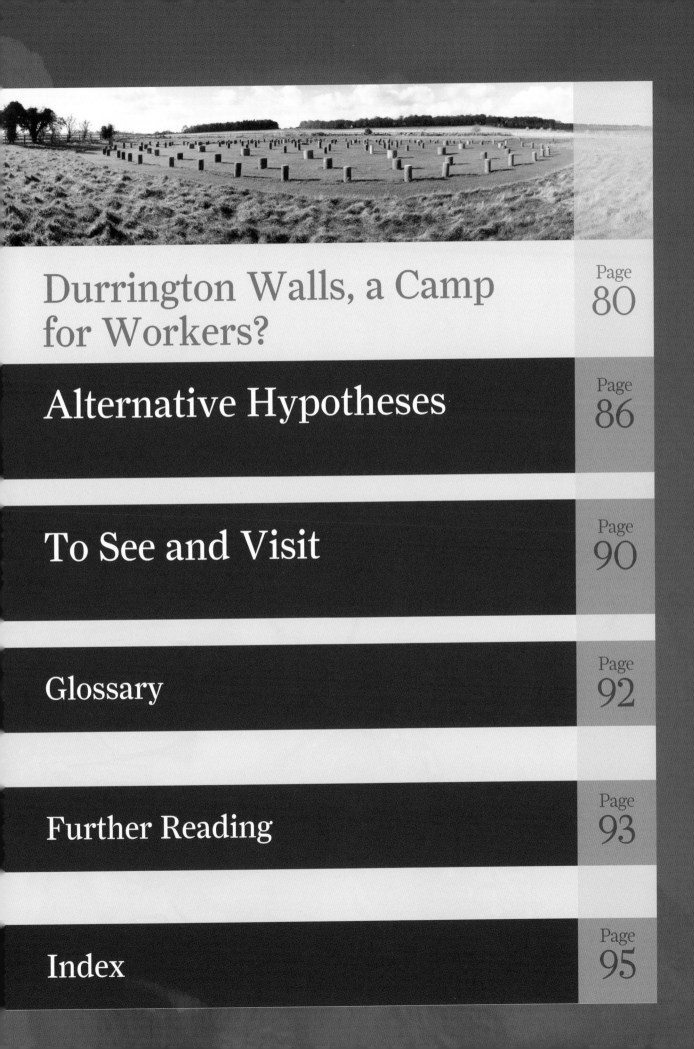

The Enduring Mystery of Machu Picchu

It was no surprise when Machu Picchu was selected in 2007 as one of "new" Seven Wonders of the World. Machu Picchu's fame has long been justified because of its superbly preserved ruins, containing some of the finest stonework of its age, perched on a sharp-edged ridge amidst a spectacular mountain landscape. There is also an air of mystery surrounding Machu Picchu that captures the imagination of all who visit it. Since it remained hidden from the outside world for centuries following the Spanish conquest of 1532 CE and there are no written records describing the site, theories are still being presented to explain why it was built and why it was abandoned.

Visitors to Machu Picchu have the rare pleasure of being able to walk among buildings little changed from the time of the Incas who lived in them. The site also allows scientists to study a virtual time capsule, for no settlement preceded Machu Picchu's construction and none followed its abandonment, thus ensuring that it was built and occupied in a span of less than 80 years – a blink of an eye in archaeological terms. Hiram Bingham, the historian/explorer who first brought Machu Picchu to the public's attention, was disappointed not to find any Inca treasure, yet his collection of bones and artifacts have enabled studies to be carried out that provide a wealth of information about Inca culture. However, the key mystery still endures: what was the meaning of the site?

Without written records, we are left only with the physical remains to help interpret Machu Picchu which has led to several imaginative theories, often lacking in solid evidence. In the case of archaeologists and historians, the focus is more on comparisons with known Inca settlements and with an analysis of the information that has come down to us about Inca beliefs.

For some scholars, it has also meant examining the site as part of a larger system, not only in relation to other Inca ruins and their ecological settings, but also to Inca religious concerns relating to important celestial bodies they worshipped and the surrounding sacred landscape. The latter has been found to be closely associated with some of the most important aspects of Inca life: the fertility of crops and animals, political control, empowerment of ritual specialists, trade and the hydrological cycle as it interacts with the celestial sphere.

Excavations within the ruins have been relatively limited since Hiram Bingham's initial investigations, but they have resulted in perhaps the most important discovery of recent times: Some 60% of the work that went into the site's construction lies underground. While these and other discoveries have changed our understanding of the site, physical changes have occurred, as well, such as the restoration work that has been undertaken. There have also been changes in the cultural use of Machu Picchu, especially with regard to the role played by what has been called "mystic tourism," where Machu Picchu has come to be seen as a place of special power and thus to attract New Agers and Andean mystics alike.

Although the best known, Machu Picchu is one of many sites located in the district of Vilcabamba. This region is known for being the last refuge of the Incas after they escaped control of the Spaniards in the 1500s. Explorers have discovered a number of Inca ruins in this region, and some of the better known sites, such as Choquequirao and Espíritu Pampa, are being restored and made more accessible to visitors.

Each visit to Machu Picchu seems to reveal something new; a previously unnoticed alignment of structures, a natural feature incorporated into the architecture, a new detail that reveals a little more about life 500 years ago. Scientists are still debating the evidence, and research will continue to provide new information that will increase our understanding of the site. However, just as we find answers to some aspects of this enigma, new questions arise. Of one thing we can be certain: Machu Picchu will remain a place of mystery for many years to come.

Johan Reinhard

An archaeologist and ethno-historian who specialized in Incan ceremonial centers and sacred grounds. Resident explorer of the National Geographic Society. Received his doctorate in Anthropology from the University of Vienna in 1974.

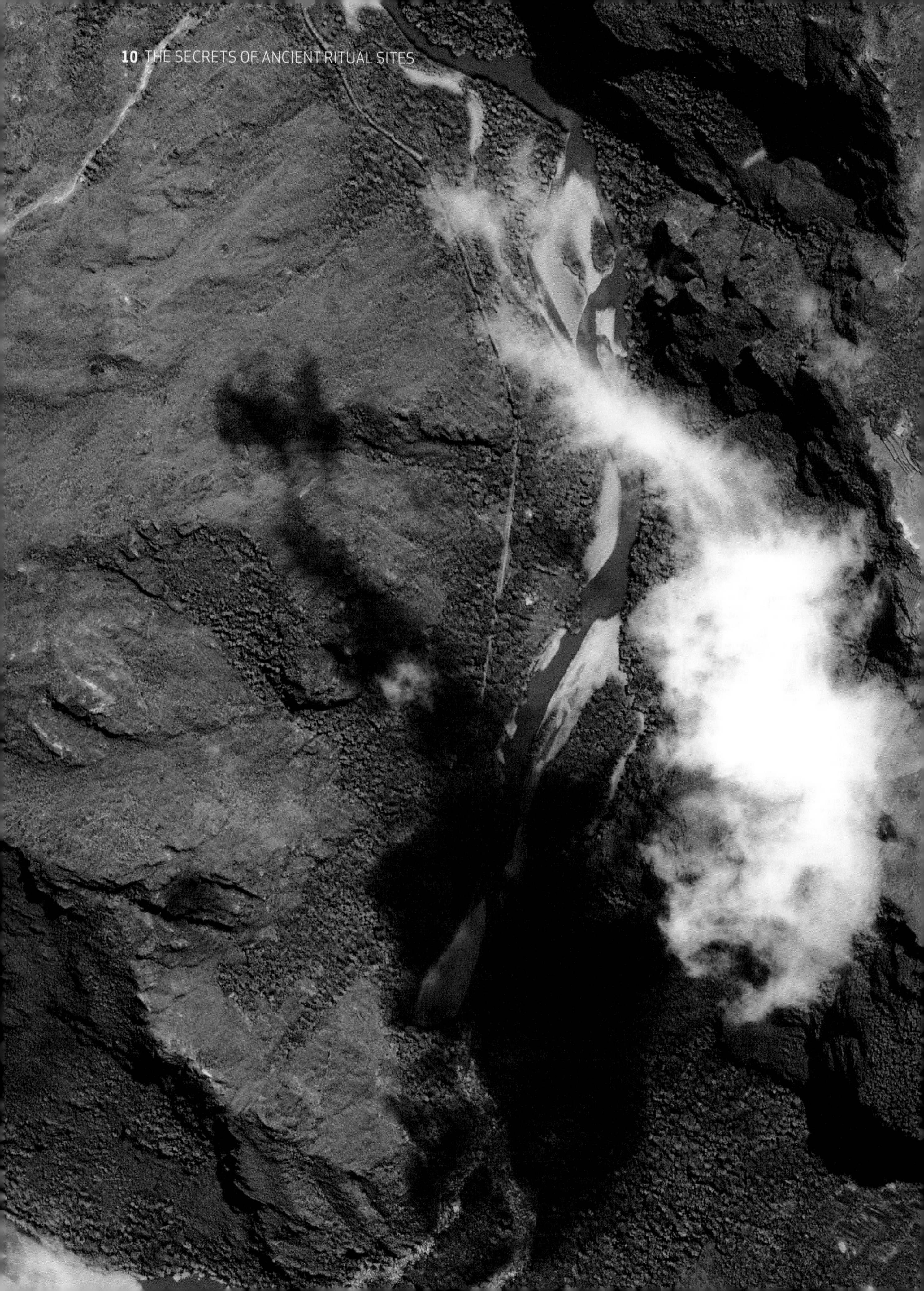

IN THE HIGHLANDS
Machu Picchu from the sky, flanked by the snaking highway and a solitary cloud.

HIDDEN
The ruins of Machu Picchu are found at 7,874 ft (2,400 m) above sea level, among the high Andean peaks and in the shadow of Huayna Picchu.

The Lost City of the Incas

In the short history of the Inca State, Machu Picchu was the sacred citadel that became stronger in the shadow of Cusco. American historian Hiram Bingham rediscovered these centuries-old ruins for the world in 1915.

Between Lake Titicaca and the Cusco valley, at the foot of the Andes, a culture was born that rapidly extended to the greater part of the Andes mountain range. At the height of its development it reached limits not even dreamed of by the other nations to follow it in ancient Peru: from Ecuador, through Peru and Bolivia to Chile and the northern part of Argentina. It was an immense territory that spanned almost 2,500 miles in length and 250 miles in width. From 10 million to 30 million people – there is disagreement about which figure is correct – came to live in the western part of South America under the control of a dynasty that entered power around the year 1200 in Cusco, "which in the native Incan language means navel of the earth," according to Inca chronicler Garcilaso de la Vega (1539–1616) in his work *Primera Parte de los Comentarios Reales de los Incas* [The Royal Commentaries of Peru] (1609). There was no mention of Machu Picchu, whose construction took place in the 15th century.

Inca culture spread freely throughout the Andean highlands. There is a legend that on the Island of the Sun, at Lake Titicaca (situated at 12,500 feet above sea level), Manco Cápac and Mama Ocllo appeared. They were the mythical founders of the Inca dynasty, and were both siblings and spouses. The legend goes on to say that Manco Cápac planted his gold staff at an altitude of 11,180 ft in the middle of an ancient settlement of Huallas, Poques and Lares, flanked by the Tullumayo and Huatanay rivers. Thus, Cusco was born and with it the so-called "legendary Inca empire," which from 1200 to 1438 had a dynasty of eight rulers: Manco Cápac, Sinchi Roca, Lloque Yupanqui, Mayta Cápac, Cápac Yupanqui, Inca Roca, Yahuar Huacac and Hatun Topa or Viracocha (who shared his name with the principal god of the Incas).

The high solitude of Machu Picchu, a jewel of Incan architecture, engineering and urban planning had not yet been constructed, but very soon it would shine. The Chanka nation threatened the

hegemonic power of the Cusco dynasty in the latter part of Viracocha's reign. Only the military resistance led by one of his sons, Yupanqui, hindered the fall of Cusco.

The ninth Inca, Pachacútec, was the first ruler of the historic Empire, the Tawantinsuyu, which in the Quechua language means "the four parts (or regions) of the world," coinciding with the four cardinal directions. During his reign Machu Picchu was constructed in secret, perhaps to preserve its priceless political or religious nature. In 1471, Pachacútec abdicated to his son Topa Inca Yupanqui: an example of a great conqueror and statesman for 22 years.

The 11th Inca, Huayna Cápac, continued the policies of his father, even though he was obligated to quash a frequent number of uprisings that occurred in his vast empire. In 1525 he died in Quito, perhaps as a result of smallpox, brought to the Americas by the Spanish conquistadors. The sickness served as advance notice of the Spanish army, which very soon would arrive to Inca lands.

CIVIL WAR

At Huayna Cápac's death, the struggle for power faced his sons, born of different women: Huáscar, who had the support of the Cusco nobility, and Atahualpa, who had the powerful northern army. In 1532, Atahualpa's troops occupied the city of Cusco and Huáscar was taken prisoner. The conqueror showed no mercy: he ordered that his brother's entire family, which to a large extent was also his own family, as well as his chiefs and personal friends, be killed. In the middle of this civil war, Spanish conquistador Francisco Pizarro, leading a group of just 200 men with some 70 horses, landed at Tumbes in April 1531. On November 15 of the following year, Atahualpa and Pizarro arranged to meet each other at Cajamarca.

At the beginning of the meeting of the two kingdoms' representatives, Dominican friar Vicente Valverde, with a cross and a book in his hands, addressed the Inca and read the "Requerimiento," an ultimatum where the indigenous people would be required to recognize the sovereignty of Castilian laws, receive envoys in peace, and accept the faith they would preach. Atahualpa smacked the book out of the friar's hand, and at Valverde's cry that "the Indian chief has thrown the book of our holy laws to the ground!" a huge artillery fire and cavalry charge began, causing the death of thousands in the Inca army. The luck of the Incas had run out.

It was for nothing that Atahualpa, taken as hostage, would offer to fill three rooms with gold and silver in exchange for his freedom. Once the ransom payment was obtained, which took months to get together, Francisco Pizarro followed the example set by Hernán Cortés with Moctezuma, the Aztec sovereign, some years before. He had the Inca garroted on August 29, 1533, for having ordered the death of his brother Huáscar, among other supposed crimes.

THE DECLINE OF THE INCAS

On November 15 of that same year, the Spanish conquerors took Cusco without opposition. The extraordinary network of Inca roads facilitated the instant success of the foreign armies. American archaeologist John Hyslop, in his book *Qhapaqñan: The Inka Road System* (1992), registered an approximate total of 14,409 miles, even though in all reality there could have been as many as 24,855 miles. It seems

▲

PLATFORMS
The classic terraces or cultivation platforms of Inca culture have a marked presence in Machu Picchu. In the picture, a channel crosses the terraces, bordered by a row of houses.

◄

ROYAL TOMB
Bingham thus named the natural cave found below the Temple of the Sun, even though no mummy was found inside. There is a staircase excavated from the rock and stones were molded in a fascinating way.

that the Spaniards did not take full advantage of the Inca roads to arrive at the heights of the sanctuary at Machu Picchu and pillage the treasures. The powerful Inca Empire had its center in Cusco, and its capture led to a quick decline. The solid political and social organization, divided between the governing-priestly nobility and the tributary-farming peasantry, was marked by its lack of strong class conflict. The social organization corresponded to linages and specific communities or to the functions that individuals within each grouping should

carry out. Machu Picchu was at the summit of the social pyramid, since it was possibly Pachacútec's vacation home and later could have become his mausoleum. A high-ranking sanctuary, offering a palace, temples and altars, as well as agricultural terraces, livestock and workshops, it is found at a unique location between two mountain peaks, abundant in water and thick vegetation, seven days' walk from the capital in Cusco. In the Tawantinsuyu – according to Peruvian anthropologist Luis E. Valcárcel in his book *Del ayllu al imperio* (1925) –

Continued on page 18 ►

The urban structure

Machu Picchu was divided into two main zones: agricultural and urban. The large main plaza was in the center of the latter. As seen in all other Inca cities, Machu Picchu had an "upper part" or *hanan* (sacred district), and a "lower part," known as the *urin* (residential district).

Imperial Residence

Most researchers agree that it was the Inca Pachacuti, founder and first sovereign of Tawantinsuyu (the Inca Empire), who ordered the construction of this citadel as a place for recreation and refuge during winter.

Location
About 73 miles from Cusco, the ancient capital of the Inca Empire, and 745 miles from Lima, the modern-day capital of Peru.

Distribution
A step, a wall and a moat, which also served as a drainage channel, separate the rural area from the urban area.

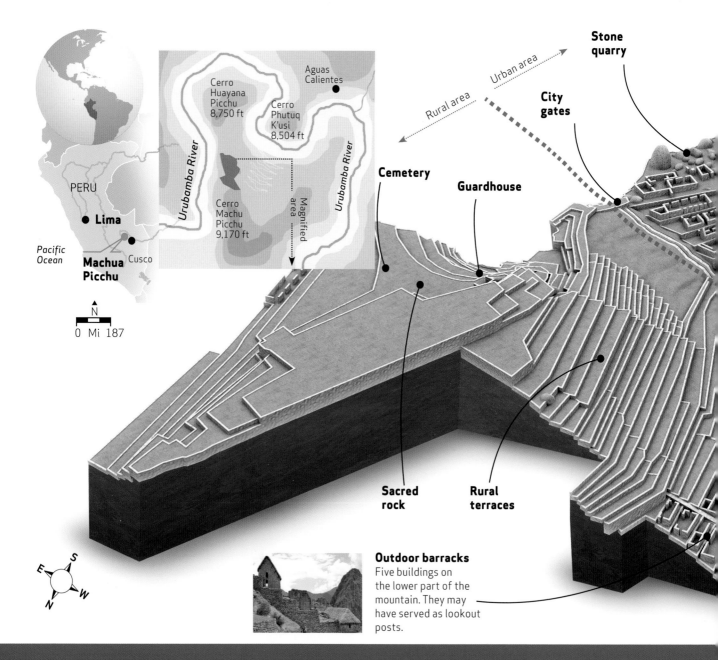

Cerro Huayana Picchu 8,750 ft

Cerro Phutuq K'usi 8,504 ft

Aguas Calientes

Urubamba River

Cerro Machu Picchu 9,170 ft

Magnified area

PERU

Lima

Pacific Ocean

Machua Picchu

Cusco

N

0 Mi 187

Stone quarry

Urban area

City gates

Rural area

Cemetery

Guardhouse

Sacred rock

Rural terraces

Outdoor barracks
Five buildings on the lower part of the mountain. They may have served as lookout posts.

enigmas

What Purpose Did the So-Called Funerary (or Ceremonial) Rock Have for Machu Picchu?

Large stones had great religious significance for the Incas. In Machu Picchu this is evident in the stones at the Temple of the Condor, the Temple of the Sun, and the Sacred Stone. Funerary Rock, also known as the Ceremonial Rock, has a polished surface with steps and a ring carved into the rock. There are theories stating this was used for mummification, but the truth is that its use is not known for certain.

Intiwuatana
"The Hitching Post of the sun" was key during the festival. Was it a solar clock, a dial to mark the position of the sun during the solstice, or a sacrificial altar?

Temple of the Three Windows

Main Temple

Priest's house

Hanan (sacred area)

Hurin (residential area)

Stone quarry

Main plaza

Group of the Three Doors
Some call it the "District of the Amautas," or teachers.

Royal tomb

Temple of the Sun
Semicircular turret; two of its windows align with the sunrise on the summer and winter solstices.

Inca Palace
The complex has dining halls, private rooms, sanitary facilities and an area for workers.

Temple of the Condor
Ceremonial center. It takes its name from an enigmatic representation at its base (below).

Group of the Mortars
Here, there are two circular fountains identified as mortars.

"agrarianism was born, which is communal property among the peasantry and worship of the sun, the universal religion."

Cusco native César Antonio Ugarte, in his work *Bosquejo de la historia económica del Perú* (1926), summed up the fundamental characteristics of the Inca economy: "Communal guardianship of the arable land by the *ayllu*, or group of related families, divided into non-transferable individual lots; communal guardianship of the water, grazing lands and forests; common cooperation in work; individual appropriation of the harvests and fruits." Philosopher Rodolfo Kusch (1922–1979) defined this system beautifully, calling it a shelter economy.

AN ABSOLUTE SOVEREIGN

The so-called Kingdom of the Sun, embodied by the Inca, the absolute sovereign, rotated spiritually around Viracocha, the creator; it followed Inti, the sun, the first of a long list of celestial gods and supernatural powers or *huacas*. These were represented by definite objects and places, which would later be erased by monotheistic Christianity and the evangelizing movement.

Everything seems to indicate that the decline of a place so carefully hidden such as Machu Picchu originated during the Spanish occupation of Cusco. It is even possible that once uninhabited, it suffered the incendiary wrath of the soldier-priests that would soon devastate the area around Vilcabamba, near the sanctuary. In the framework of the Spanish empire in America, the so-called "General idolatry inspector" was the person responsible for visiting the natives to exhort them to leave their polytheistic culture and denounce sinners. Jesuit Pablo Joseph de Arteaga (1564–1622), who was appointed as the inspector and wrote *La extirpación de la idolatría en el Perú* [The removal of idolatry in Peru] shared a typical day's work: "all of the

mallquis (the pagan bodies the Indians worshiped), and we found many of these, we burned. Among them two pairs of small silver cups were found, with which it appeared the Indians used to drink to the dead. At nightfall, we gave thanks to the Lord for our successes, having taken all of the idols and everything else we found." Other idolatry eradicators in the search for huacas, mallquis, *conopas* (small stone statues for divine offerings) acted with much less consideration. Indian chronicler Felipe Huaman Poma de Ayala, author of *Nueva crónica y buen gobierno* [New chronicle and good government] (1639), interpreted for the visit of Cristóbal de Albornoz. Even though he defended these idolatry eradication campaigns, he censured the abuses committed in their name.

THE INCA RESISTANCE

The majority of rebel Inca forces took refuge in Vilcabamba, led by Manco Inca Yupanqui, son of Huayna Cápac, who besieged Cusco for 12 months and established his general headquarters in Tambo, today Ollantaytambo, at the gates of the Tawantinsuyu capital. This focus of Inca resistance, which at the death of Manco Inca Yupanqui, came to be led by his sons Tito Cusi and Túpac Amaru, lasted for the better part of 40 years. In 1572, viceroy Francisco of Toledo ordered the final assault of Spanish troops on Vilcabamba, and had Túpac Amaru decapitated in the Cusco Plaza and nailed his head to a stake. Thus the Tawantinsuyu came to its end. Vilcabamba became a place of Inca myth, but also one of the most sought after places by adventurers, explorers and writers, the majority from Europe and the United States. American Hiram Bingham (1875–1956), associate professor of South American History at Yale University, arrived at this remote region for the first time in 1909. He is famed for having covered on foot a good part of South America. In 1906,

Antonio Raimondi
1826–1890

Naturalist born in Milan, Italy. Arrived at Peru in 1850 and dedicated himself to the scientific study of the country, covering archaeology to zoology, the arts to chemistry, and paleontology to geography. Among his archaeological studies, the work carried out at the pre-Inca site Chavín de Huántar is worth mentioning. He traveled for almost 20 years all over Peru, covering a total of 28,000 miles. Even though he died before the discovery of Machu Picchu, his studies helped to establish a basis for better understanding of pre-Colombian cultures in Peru.

FORERUNNER Raimondi's influence on scientific knowledge of Peru is without measure. His greatest work is *El Perú*, in six volumes.

María Rostworowski
1915

Daughter of a Polish father and a Peruvian mother, she is a leading expert on the Inca and other ancient Peruvian cultures. She studied with historian Raúl Porras Barrenechea, and her first work was dedicated to the Inca Pachacuti, who ordered the construction of Machu Picchu.

EXPERT Rostworowski's work has provided a richer and more complete view of the Incas.

◀ *Continued from page 15*　　　*Continued on page 22* ▶

Hiram Bingham

Son and grandson of Protestant missionaries, Bingham was born in Honolulu, Hawaii, in 1875. Even though he earned degrees from three universities (Yale, California, and Harvard), he never formally studied archaeology. In an expedition sponsored by Yale University, in 1911 he rediscovered Machu Picchu, as well as three other important archaeological sites from the Sacred Valley of the Incas (Choquequirao, Vitcos, and Vilcabamba). He erroneously believed that Machu Picchu was the last capital of the Incas, and that Vilcabamba was a minor site, when actually the reverse was true. He published *Lost City of the Incas* in 1948, a work dedicated to his expedition to Machu Picchu, and a best seller from its first printing. After his field work, he dedicated himself to politics: he was governor-elect for Connecticut (he only served one day) for the Republican Party and a member of the U.S. Senate. The widely known movie personality Indiana Jones was inspired by him.

DISCOVERER Bingham was not the first person to walk around Machu Picchu since the era of the Conquest. His great success was making the existence of this mysterious place known to the world and motivating archaeological investigation thereof.

1875–1956

"Without the slightest expectation of finding anything more interesting than the stone-faced terraces, I finally left the cool shade of the pleasant little hut and climbed farther up the ridge."
H. B.

Johan Reinhard
1943

Born in Illinois. Specialist in pre-Colombian archaeology, as well as an expert mountain climber. Responsible for some of the most significant discoveries of Andean mummies, among them that of Juanita (and three others) at the Ampato volcano, Peru (1995) and the three Niños [Children] del Llullaillaco, in Salta, Argentina (1999). He published, in 1991, *Machu Picchu: The Sacred Center*, where he presented innovative theories about this archaeological site.

INNOVATOR Aside from his notable field discoveries, Johan Reinhard has suggested various theories about the locations of Inca sites.

Terraces and construction

The urban sector of Machu Picchu was for the nobility and has various temples and sacred areas. The agricultural district on the other hand was wholly dedicated to the crop cultivation. Despite the high number of terraces, all signs indicate that Machu Picchu was not self-sufficient.

Terraces

The rural area was made up of large terraces or platforms with crops located on the side of the mountain.

▬ Upper terraces
▬ Lower terraces
▬ Urban area

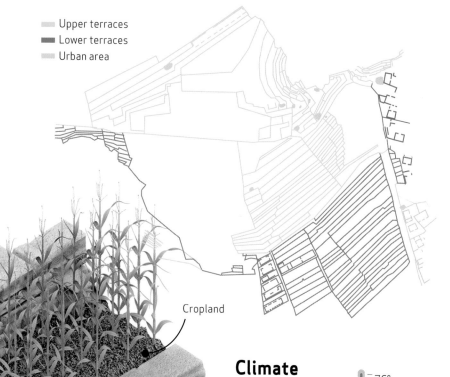

BREAKDOWN OF A PLATFORM

Retaining Wall

Cropland

Fill
Comprising large and small stones, gravel, clay and fertile soil. It facilitated drainage, preventing water from collecting and compromising its structure.

Side of the mountain

Function
The use of terraces enabled the Inca to cultivate crops on hillsides and avoid erosion caused by rainwater. It is believed that they also served for protection.

Climate

As Machu Picchu is located in a mountainous area, the climate is warm during the day and cool at night. It rains frequently, especially between November and March.

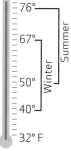

76°
67°
50°
40°
32° F

Winter
Summer

Retaining Wall

Steps of embedded rocks

Irrigation

Cropland was nourished using rainwater. The water channels that descended from the slopes were used by the urban area and the ceremonial fountains.

What Was the Importance of the Location of the Farming Terraces?

enigmas

Even though the agricultural sector covers half the surface area of the complex, it is calculated that it could only feed about 55 people, while the permanent population was at least 300. A recent examination of the terraces shows that they farmed high value crops, like special varieties of corn and medicinal plants. It has also been speculated that this was an area for experimentation with crops that would later be cultivated on a larger scale in other areas.

Main building complex

- Workshops, housing and the city's gates
- Temple of the Sun, Royal Tomb
- Royal Residence
- Sacred Square (Temple of the Three Windows, Main Temple)
- Intihuatana
- Sacred Rock
- Group of the Three Doors
- Group of the Mortars
- Group of the Condor

Hanan

Hurin

0   164 ft   328

N

Distribution

In Hanan, there was a Royal Tomb, the district of the Amautas and the mortars, the Royal Palace and the Intihuatana. In Hurin, the Group of Three Doors, the Temple of the Condor, the Turret (or Temple of the Sun) and the Acllahuasi can be found.

Architecture

When building, the Inca considered the position of the sun during the solstices.

Roofs

A wooden structure was erected on top of the stone; layers of straw were placed on top of this.

The significant amount of rain that fell in the region made it necessary for roofs to be slanted to prevent water from accumulating. This made it possible for rainwater to run off easily.

63°

Walls

Walls of stone were joined up by using mud mortar. All the material was sourced from the quarries of the complex.

Lithic bolts

The logs that made up the roof's frame were fastened using ropes tied to stone bolts.

Foundations

Pilasters and dividing walls were sunk to make them sturdier.

Stone colonnade

Before Bingham

Even though it is still unknown whether Spanish conquerors arrived at Machu Picchu and, if they had, why they would have passed over it, it is a fact that a number of people arrived at Machu Picchu before Bingham. This does not include the local farmers, who used the terraces for their domestic crops. Almost a decade before Bingham's arrival, landowner and Cusco native Agustín Lizárraga found the site. As a testimony to his find, he left the date of his visit written on one of the walls, something that Bingham noted in his diary ("by some scribbles made on the wall of one of the most beautiful buildings, we realized that the ruins had been visited in 1901 by Lizárraga, landowner of the area surrounding the San Miguel bridge").

Toward mid-2008, American cartographer Paolo Greer announced that there was evidence the city had been found (and pillaged) by a German adventurer named Augusto Berns, in 1867 (more than 40 years before Bingham), with the approval of the Peruvian government. The evidence consists of a series of maps and registries, and it is believed that while there, Berns methodically extracted the treasures of the Inca ruins. This would explain why Bingham found pieces of huge historical and archaeological value but little in the way of riches. However, Greer's announcement is surrounded by controversy. Peruvian historian Mariana Mould de Pease reported that she had already revealed this information in a book of hers in 2003 and that she herself provided Greer with a large part of the data he presented to support his case.

LATE ARRIVAL
Hiram Bingham's men explore Machu Picchu. Bingham made the ruins known worldwide, but others were there ahead of him.

Machu Picchu: not that unknown

In his work *Historia General del Qosqo* (1992), Peruvian historian José Tamayo Herrera referred to a text dated August 8, 1776, made public by Cusco native and indigenous educator José Uriel García (1894–1965), to show that Machu Picchu was not an unknown site. According to the text, the Ochoa brothers paid 350 pesos to Mrs. Manuela Almirón Villegas for the "sites of Pijchu, Machupijchu and Huaynapijchu" which they, in turn, sold in 1782 to Spanish Chief Magistrate of the Urubamba Valley, Marco Antonio de la Cámara.

MISSING TREASURE
It is likely that valued treasures from Machu Picchu were taken away before Bingham's arrival.

he walked from Venezuela to Colombia, following the same Andean route taken by Simón Bolívar in 1819. Two years later, he followed the old commerce route used by the Spaniards, from Buenos Aires to Lima, through the Andes. His Peruvian adventure took him to the remains of a place called Choquequirao, which according to his native guides had been the last capital of the Inca rebel forces. The lost city of the Incas had always awakened the greed of men who

◀ Continued from page 18

traveled the area around Vilca-bamba with the hope of finding lost treasures. In 1710, Spanish explorer Juan Arias Díaz Cañete had stated "the news is true that by old traditions the riches of these areas can be had." But Bingham could see that Choquequirao was not the place they were looking for. In 1911, the historian returned to Cusco as director of an archaeological expedition for Yale University and entered the Urubamba Valley to finally discover the lost city. At last, on the morning of June 24 of

that same year, accompanied by a sergeant of the civil guard named Carrasco, he climbed the cultivation terraces of farmers Melquíades Richarte and Anacleto Álvarez, who lived there with their family. Richarte's son, Pablito, led them to the ruins covered in vegetation where he used to play, named Machu Picchu (and in Quechua, pronounced "machu pikchu"). In 1912 and 1915, Bingham, with support from Yale University and the National Geographic Society, returned to the heights of

Machu Picchu with a team of experts in various fields to conduct excavations. Bing-ham decided to believe that Machu Picchu had been the last stronghold of the Inca resistance. Today it is known this was not the case. It was a royal residence, a sanctuary, a fortress and finally, a lost city, hidden from the eyes of the world. Its discovery opened a world of unknowns, many of which still remain unanswered. The more Machu Picchu is studied, the more mysterious it becomes.

▲

CHECKPOINT
The "house of the guard," with its rebuilt roof, is an excellent place to begin a tour of Machu Picchu. From there the city is captured in view, with the summit of Huayna Picchu serving as a backdrop.

Access to Machu Picchu

From high up, a panoramic view allows observation of the distinct roads leading to the hidden Inca city. The Inca Trail, from Cusco to Machu Picchu, is the most well-known. In 1998 a side path was discovered that connects the citadel to the Urubamba River.

 MODERN ROAD
The winding Hiram Bingham Highway unites the village of Aguas Calientes with the city of Machu Picchu (5 mi). A bus ascends the rocky and steep, zigzag trail. Bingham attended the inauguration of the road bearing his name in 1948.

 THE INCA ROUTE
Various archaeological sites mark this road, which connects Cusco with Machu Picchu. An outline of

Centennial paths

The vast network of Inca roads extends for some 15,500 miles from Cusco, the capital, to the four parts of the Tawantinsuyu. Since the vast majority of the paths existed before the Incas, they often only had to improve what was there already. The *chasquis*, or Inca couriers, would run at high speeds on this network of roads to deliver messages.

3

How Was Machu Picchu Built?

The city was constructed under the direction of the Inca Pachacuti, founder of the Tawantinsuyu. It is a master work of Inca architecture, a huge monument of stone in the middle of a majestic natural landscape.

The citadel of Machu Picchu was built on the sloping land of the Vilcabamba mountain range, flanked by the meandering Urubamba River. The builders had to adapt to the abrupt topography of the area, with almost vertical slopes and deep gorges, something commonly found in most of Inca settlements in the mountain range, hence the tiered constructions of terraces. In Machu Picchu the trees had to be cut down and a set of platforms built with irrigation channels to facilitate the cultivation of crops (mainly corn and coca, as well as other fruits and tubers). The upper platforms sometimes reached 66 feet in length, having support walls of 7–13 feet high. The construction material used most by the Incas was stone. Diorite, porphyry and especially granite were the two most common.

EXCELLENT STONEWORK

Machu Picchu stands out for the high quality of the stonework seen there. The manner of shaping the stones (sometimes colossal in size) and the perfect wall adjustments, both on the surface and laterally, caused great admiration and amazement among the Spaniards. The architects and builders must have been professionals working for the State. The work – carried out by forced labor or shift workers – was completed by thousands of stonecutters who pounded stones with other harder ones. To transport the huge blocks from the quarry to the work area, the cords of ropes with which they were tied had to be pulled a distance of approximately 20 miles. They were dragged on wooden rollers, and stone ramps were used to raise them up. Small stones could be transported on the backs of both llamas and men. The wheel had no practical use in America. Its use was probably limited due to the little help it would provide in a mountainous, rocky terrain without the possibility of using strong draft animals. With regard to construction techniques, the plumb was used, as well as other instruments for leveling and measuring angles and distances; hammers and stone axes were the basic tools used. Once the rocks arrived at the work site, the blocks were crafted and smoothed. Using an erosion process, perhaps putting sand into the cracks and gaps, they tried to modify one block to the next until their respective surfaces would be perfectly matched.

Polishing the Stones

The procedure for giving the stones their desired shape was a simple but laborious one, requiring a lot of time.

1 EXTRACTION
Wooden wedges were placed and inserted in the cracks of the stone to widen them.

2 SOFTENING
Water was poured onto the wood to expand it and deepen the crack until the rock separated.

3 POLISHING
The stone was tapped to smooth its surface, and then it was polished with sand and water to give it a better finish.

Was Machu Picchu a Sanctuary?

There are documents that verify the close relationship that Pachacuti felt with the lands upon which Machu Picchu was built. It was his place of solace and rest during his reign, and later a sacred location where his mummy would be venerated.

In the shadow of the far mountain Salcantay 20,574 ft, considered as the *apu* or "greater spirit," and the nearby Huayna Picchu (8,750 ft), among other sacred peaks, the heights of Machu Picchu transmitted the unique vibrations of Inca worship of the dead, and especially of the Tawantinsuyu founder, Pachacuti. Spanish chronicler Juan de Betanzos (1510–1576), in his work *Suma y narración de los incas* (1551), provided firsthand accounts about the relationship between the first Inca of the Tawantinsuyu and Machu Picchu, supported by the testimony of his wife Angelina Coya Yupanqui, a member of Inca nobility and one of Pachaccuti's descendants. Thus, it was confirmed that his mummy was located in a village called Patallacta, which he himself had had built. Even though in the area there were many *patallacta*, a Quechua word meaning "village in the heights," Betanzos may very well have been referring to Machu Picchu.

PLACE OF REST

Machu Picchu – Pachacti's patallacta – seems to have been his vacation home before it became his mausoleum. Chronicler Betanzos makes it known that the mummy of the Inca used to be carried to the city of Cusco for the celebration of certain festivals. Once it was placed in the Coricancha (Temple of the Sun) with the "forms" (mummies) of the other rulers, it was an active participant in the ritual worship of dead Incas, initiated by Pachacuti himself. Ceremonies for the living and dead were held, as if there were no difference, and there were songs, stories of military engineering feats, food, drink, and even clothing changes. Once returned to the sanctuary of Machu Picchu, the mummy was restored to the Royal Tomb, located below the Torreón, which was a huge stone and had two trapezoidal windows that served as a solar observatory. From June 21–24 – the winter solstice in the Southern Hemisphere – the rays of the sun entered in through the windows of this temple: it was the herald of the new agricultural cycle. In this unique space, also known as the Temple of the Sun, there could also be found the House of the Ñusta, perhaps an *acllahuasi* ("house of the chosen virgins").

In Machu Picchu, the Inca Pachacuti would have been in the company of only those clos-

In the Image of Nature

enigmas

Some investigators have pointed out the possibility that the Incas would often sculpt inspired by the nearby natural forms. As seen in the picture, the sacred rock known as Intiwatana could be a copy of the form of the mountain Huayna Picchu, which is found behind it. Nearby is the compound of the Sacred Stone, marked by a monolithic piece which also appears to be a carbon copy of the mountains in front of it. From this stone, heading west by means of a steep path with steps carved in the rock and which crosses small agricultural terraces, the summit of Huayna Picchu can be reached. There in the heights of the "young mountain" a large stone can be seen in the shape of a throne, known as the "Inca chair." From this point, there is an incomparable view of the sanctuary, the Urubamba canyon and the sacred mountains. On the north side, the mountain houses a cavern, similar to the royal tomb at the Temple of the Sun, connected to another further up which has stones, trapezoidal niches and alcoves. This grouping of caves is known as the Temple of the Moon.

Is Machu Picchu in Line With Other Cities?

In recent decades, the symbolic importance of the Inca site locations has been emphasized, as well as the existence of a relationship between the main cities constructed by them. Mathematician and archaeologist María Scholten d'Ebneth discovered in 1977 that Cajamarca, Machu Picchu, Ollantaytambo, Cusco and Tiwanaku appear aligned in a northwest-southeast direction, in a diagonal line of sacred value that is present in numerous crafts and Andean objects. This line has been called "Viracocha's Route," relating it to the mythical path taken by the Andean creator god from Tiwanaku to the Pacific Ocean.

THE INTIWATANA
Its elevated location makes this stone an optimal place for astronomical observations.

est to him: the *coya* (main wife), the *panaca* (the royal family), the *amautas* (wise men) and other servants.

Using the streets, the four plazas, the terraces and the 3,000 stairs, one could arrive at any temple, palace or sacred rock in the urban sector, where the noise of the channeled water could be heard. Between the Main Temple, opening on the Central Plaza, and the Inca Palace there were fountains that started at the summits, descended through stone aqueducts and jumped from one terrace to another. The priestly body was grouped around the Main Temple and the Temple of Three Windows, composed of huge polyhedrons, finely sculpted and assembled to perfection. According to Bingham, who was responsible for naming most of the buildings, these three windows were related to the myth of the origin of the Incas.

MOVING THE MUMMIES

The amautas, the philosophers or wise men for the Inca nation, lived in the Intellectuals District. It is an area dominated by structures with high walls and reddish stones, beautiful windows, alcoves and lithic nails protruding in the shape of a cylinder. On the ground there are various circular stone mortars used for making various dyes for ceramics and fabrics.

Some researches suggest that it was the amautas who decided to move the mummy of Pachacuti away from Machu Picchu – where around 400 people dedicated to worshiping the dead Inca lived – along with the mummies of his main wife and other members of the royal family, together with their treasures, before the arrival of the Spanish. This was a wise move, also applied to the mummies of the sovereigns resting in the Cusco Coricancha. However, archaeologist Luis G. Lumbreras stated: "The Spanish mounted an aggressive search for the mummies of the Incas. Polo de Ondegardo, also a chronicler, found, at the request of the Viceroy Marquis of Cañete, the bodies of Pachacuti, Huayna Cápac and his wife, Mama Ocllo, in a house in Cusco. The bodies were then buried, according to the dictates of Catholic doctrine, in San Andrés, a hospital in Barrios Altos, Lima."

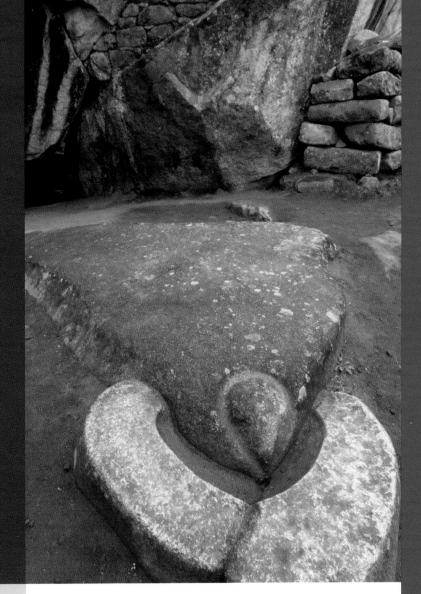

THREE WINDOWS

In spite of its name, the Temple of the Three Windows originally had five openings; those on either end were filled in and converted into niches by the Incas themselves. The windows are the largest ever constructed by the Incas: they measure 6.2 ft high. Between the windows, ceramic fragments were found, which could indicate the ceremonial breaking of vessels and keros.

TEMPLE OF THE CONDOR

The Temple of the Condor owes its name to a rock barely protruding from the ground which has the appearance of a condor drinking from a circular fountain. It contains numerous underground passages and water sources. Until recently it was believed that this area functioned as a prison for delinquents, but today this hypothesis is considered highly improbable.

The *Torreón* or Temple of the Sun

This is the only circular structure at Machu Picchu, and it functioned as a solar observatory. Its architecture represents some of the finest work of all Inca construction. Under the building there is a grotto (the Royal Tomb) where apparently the mummy of the Inca Pachacuti rests. Also from there is a water source that supplies 16 other springs.

The top of the Intiwatana, "the hitching post of the Sun," is accessed by a "staircase" of 78 levels. Located on a hill surrounded by various terraces and platforms, this sacred site is a granite block carved in various planes and crowned by a four-sided prism that seems to reflect and complement the shape of the "new mountain" (Huayna Picchu) in front of it. Some investigators think this was a gnomonic object: an astronomy instrument to measure time, determined by the height of the sun according to the direction and the projected shadow.

From Intiwatana, Chilean poet and Nobel Prize winner Pablo Neruda metaphorically saw the whole of America and was inspired with the original idea for his *Canto General* (1950). He had traveled to the Inca ruins by mule in October 1943, but could never have imagined the sanctuary hiding behind the stones. Before writing *Las Alturas de Macchu Picchu* (The Heights of Macchu Picchu) he stated: "I wanted to touch on the theme of death for the last time. In the loneliness of the ruins, death can never be far from one's thoughts."

The Ceremony of the Sun

June 21 – the shortest day of the year – was the most important day for the Incas. That day they celebrated the Festival of the Sun, dedicated to the god Inti. The ceremony, closely tied with their agricultural needs, included a strict ritual, with fasts and abstinence in the days leading up to the festival.

Natural cycles

Since they were an agrarian society, the Incas had to have exact knowledge of the cycles of nature. It is not strange, therefore, that the winter solstice, which in the Southern Hemisphere happens on June 21, was aptly named the Festival of the Sun and became the most important Inca celebration. The festival lasted for several days and included processions, dances, songs and animal sacrifices to ensure a good harvest season. The illustration depicts how this festival might have looked in Machu Picchu.

The Winter Solstice

In Machu Picchu, during the winter solstice, the rays of the sun would go through the east window of the Temple of the Sun (also called the Torreón). The solar rays would fall on the sacred rock which occupied almost all of the enclosure. An intentional cut in said rock, which marked the rays streaming in through the window, proves that the Inca temple was an astronomical observatory.

KEY LOCATIONS FOR THE FESTIVAL OF THE SUN

1 ENTRANCE
The llamas, carrying foodstuffs and various items for the festivities, entered through the main gate toward the storehouses.

2 INTIWATANA
"The hitching post of the sun" was fundamental in the celebration of the winter solstice. A stairway of 78 stairs unites this location with the Main Square.

3 UNFINISHED TEMPLE
An area for worship in the initial stages of construction remained unfinished due to the abrupt abandonment of the city.

4 MAIN SQUARE
The only open space of the complex. This is where the festivities took place, and it was also the meeting place in Machu Picchu.

5 TEMPLE OF THE SUN
Restricted use, exclusively for royalty. The layout of the construction indicated the arrival of the winter solstice.

Who Were the Virgins of the Sun?

A select group of women, of royal blood and chosen for their beauty, took a vow of chastity to become wives of the sun god. These women were the Virgins of the Sun, a term coined by the Spanish conquistadors.

The Virgins of the Sun lived in the city of Cusco, more or less where the Convent of Saint Catherine, of the Dominican order, stands today. Some historians from the colonial period used this term for all women living in the *acllahausi* (residence of chosen women), whose primary edifice in Cusco served as a model for those built in other important cities throughout Tawantinsuyu. However, it is worth the trouble to make a distinction here. It was under the Inca ruler Pachacuti that the body of *acllas*, or "chosen women," was created: this group was linked to the priestly nobility. An exclusively feminine institution, it depended on the State for its subsistence and new members; it came into being at the same time as the cult of Inti, the sun god, at the Coricancha temple in Cusco.

The process of selecting acllas was the responsibility of specific officials (the *apu panaca*), who periodically traveled throughout the territory in search of girls 8 to 12 years old, chosen for their extreme beauty and unquestioned virginity, generally the daughters of provincial chieftains or the chieftains of Cusco. They were then locked up in the acllahuasi, where they learned to weave, sew, cook, make *chicha* (an alcoholic drink made from corn fermented in sugar water) and other high-level domestic tasks.

AT THE SERVICE OF THE INCA

The Inca leader disposed of these women as he wished, making them concubines or gifting them as virgins to illustrious nobles and warriors, who were permitted to practice polygamy.

But the Virgins of the Sun were another matter. Their entire lives were dedicated to the service of the sun god and caring for the Incan mummies. In addition to making clothes for deities and priests, they prepared the sacred chicha and *zancu*, a type of bread made with corn and the blood of Andean camelids, which served as a divine offering during the Inti Raymi festivals in June, the month when sacrifices were made to the sun. Peruvian archaeologist Federico Kauffmann Doig, author of the classic *Manual de arqueología peruana* (Manual of Peruvian Archaeology, 1978), observed: "Only a small group of acllas were chosen to remain forever in the acllahuasi. They were called *mamacona*, and the role of these older acllas was to instruct the novices, run the acllahuasi, and act as priestesses. As they took a vow of eternal chastity, they were called 'Virgins of the Sun' by the Spaniards, a term they used for all acllas."

Mostly Feminine

The excavations performed in 1912 and 1915 by the team under Hiram Bingham, which did not include a single archaeologist, revolved around the search for tombs and palaces. They discovered 107 tombs, of which 52 were exhumed under the direction of an osteologist from Yale University, George F. Eaton, while the rest were exhumed by locals Melquíades Richarte and Anacleto Álvarez, who lived near Machu Picchu. After realizing that most of the human remains found were female, Bingham proposed the following theory: that the sacred place had been the final home of the hundred

Virgins of the Sun, who took refuge in the mountains of Vilcabamba before the fall of Cusco at the hands of the Spanish conquistadors. Peruvian archaeologist Luis G. Lumbreras referenced documents from the 16th century that spoke of thousands of mamaconas established in the Urubamba Valley. He added: "Regarding Picchu, they clearly state that the land in this region was in the service of the cult of the dead, in memory of the Incan Pachacuti, who owned the land. These documents also state that the women and workers in the imperial palaces were mostly *mitmacuna*, that is, colonists."

What Was Life in the *Acllahuasi* Like?

The acllas were always locked up, and no one could see them except the Inca leader's wife (the *coya*) and her daughters, sent by the Inca leader to see whether or not everything was in order, or if they needed anything. As a result, the acllas only interacted among themselves. The home of the Virgins of the Sun was at the end of a narrow passage traversing the entire acllahuasi. There were men responsible for security and other special tasks, usually outside the cloister area. These men were known as *punku kamayu*. Giving in to carnal desire or inappropriate behavior inexorably led them to death.

MAMACONA
Statuette of a Virgin of the Sun (above) found in a mountain-top sanctuary. Right, a reconstruction illustrating how a chosen maiden or mamacona was viewed. Sometimes they were sacrificed as part of the ritual called *capacocha*.

CEREMONIAL VASE
The food and drink destined for ceremonies to honor the god Inti were prepared in the acllahuasi. *Queros* were pitchers for drink offerings and other rituals.

Were the Inca Mummies Child Sacrifices?

Human sacrifice was the most sacred Inca ritual, one that was only performed in the most solemn moments. The best offering was physically perfect children. Some were destined for the "high sanctuaries," or snowy mountain peaks.

In historical accounts from the 16th century, the use of the word "package" could be deceptive. What is certain is that most of the time it referred to a mummified body (*mallqui*, a Quechua word meaning "seed" and "ancestor"), especially in reference to the Inca. All deceased lords were subject to a permanent preservation procedure that took place daily, which included washing with grass and oils, a change of clothes, food, protection from insects, adoration, preparation of a litter to carry the body to Qurikancha or the Temple of the Sun, and a celebration in Cusco's Central Plaza from dawn to midday, if time permitted. Conquistador and historian Pedro de Pizarro (1514–1571) described the ritual in his *Relaciones del descubrimiento y conquista de los reinos del Perú*

(History of the Discovery and Conquering of the Kings of Peru): "Every day, all the people gathered in the plaza, seated in rings according to age, and everyone ate together; they placed firewood, that had been cut to exact lengths and was very dry, in front of the dead; once lit, the fire burned food that had been placed there, so the dead ate the same as everyone else. They also placed large pitchers of chicha (wine) before the dead, pouring out the wine after showing it to them, the dead sharing the pitchers with the dead, then the living, who shared them with the dead..."

OFFERINGS TO THE GODS

A document from 1568 mentions that the inhabitants of Picchu paid tribute to the Spaniards with coca, and that during the height of the Inca empire, "what they gathered

was used to perform sacrifices and rites to the dead, as was the custom between them in this kingdom." American anthropologist Johan Reinhard went somewhat further, and higher, to discover, between 1995 and 1999, 14 human sacrifices at various archaeological sites located on the peaks of five Andean mountains. His first expedition was to snow-covered Ampato (20,699 ft) in Peru, and his last was to the top of Llullaillaco (22,110 ft) in Argentina. Reinhard found frozen mummies of both boys and girls, with various offerings. Other burial platforms, visited by daring grave robbers, were empty. In one of them, a thick layer of volcanic ash was found. This led archaeologists to conjecture that the Incas offered sacrifices on the mountain peaks in response to active volcano eruptions.

Capacocha

In the human sacrifice known as *capacocha* (power of the water), children less than ten years old were offered by royal obligation, destined for the Sun, the Moon, the Inca dead and the reigning lord. According to historian Cristóbal de Molina el Cuzqueño, a mixed-race priest from Cusco who wrote *Fábulas y ritos de los Incas* (Legends and Rites of the Incas), the blood of these children was used to mark the mummy's face, and "they gave [the blood] to idols, covering the body, and also spilled it on the ground as part of the ceremony." Death was usually caused by an accurate blow to the head.

REST WITHOUT PEACE
The exhibition of Inca mummies has caused controversy between scientists, tourists, and the descendants of the peoples in question.

Maybe They Weren't Human Sacrifices?

Katia Gibaja, a descendant of the Quechua and head of the Andean Information Branch of the Museum of High Altitude Archaeology in Salta (MAAM, as abbreviated in Spanish), makes it clear that the concept of "sacrifice" does not exist in the Quechua language. With the arrival of the Spanish invaders, "burying their loved ones on the high mountains was how they protected them from death. They believed that someday, in some way, they would awaken."

High Altitude Archaeology

Cemeteries on High

Mountaintop burials are another of the surprising feats of the Incas, as some of them have been found at heights surpassing 20,000 feet (6,000 meters). The Incas reached these heights some 400 years before modern climbers for the purpose of performing the ritual known as capacocha (human sacrifice, usually of children) on the chosen mountain peaks, a sublimely sacred act. The children, from any place in Tawantinsuyu, were carried in a solemn ceremony from Cusco to their final destination. American archaeologist and mountaineer Johan Reinhard was the leader of the team that found the mummy Juanita in 1995 on Mount Ampato in Peru, and three mummified children in 1999 on the volcano Llullaillaco in Argentina.

PLACE OF BURIAL

CAMP ONE

BASE CAMP

Route to the Top

The Llullaillaco expedition took place in three stages: the climb to base camp, at 16,000 ft; from base camp to Camp One, at 20,000 ft; and from Camp One to the place of burial, at 22,000 ft, virtually on the summit (22,100 ft).

LLULLAILLACO EXPEDITION

1 EXCAVATION
Once at the site, the Reinhard expedition began the excavation using archaeological tools and techniques. Accessing the remains was very difficult.

2 DISINTERMENT
Once the three mummies had been located, Reinhard and his team proceeded to carefully uncover them. They discovered that the state of preservation was almost perfect.

3 PROTECTION
To protect the hundreds of years old bodies and keep them intact, the team wrapped the mummies in snow and foam rubber sheets.

4 DESCENT
During descent, the mummies were strapped to the archaeologist's backs. Trucks full of dry ice then transported the mummies to their final destination in the city of Salta.

The Mummies of Llullaillaco

The three mummies found rest in the Museum of High Altitude Archaeology in Salta, in cryo-preservation chambers at a temperature of -2°F, similar to that of the mountain peak. Only one mummy at a time is on display, and they are rotated roughly every six months.

LIGHTNING GIRL
Named thus because her body was struck by lightning sometime after her death, she was only 6 years old.

THE MAIDEN
She is believed to have been about 15 years old. She wore a wool headdress with white feathers that is now exhibited separately.

THE BOY
He was found tied up with his head between his knees. He was about 7 years old, and there is evidence of blood on his clothes.

Temperature control

The mummy Juanita, preserved in a museum in Arequipa, Peru, is displayed in a glass capsule with steel edges. Its temperature is maintained at a constant -2°F (-19°C), thanks to a preservation system consisting of a modified packaged terminal air conditioner (PTAC), specially developed by the company Carrier.

ORNAMENTS
A metal plate adorned Lightning Girl's head. The lightning strike left her face exposed on the mountain peak.

HAIR
The hair was carefully combed, and two thin braids come down over the forehead. Some two dozen artifacts were found near the body.

SMOOTH SKIN
Despite having been struck by lightning on her shoulder, chest and ear, Lightning Girl's skin was extraordinarily well-preserved.

What Caused the Citadel's Decline?

The taking of Cusco by the Spaniards in November of 1533 marked the end of Machu Picchu's decadence. After 1550, now uninhabited, it may have been burned during a military expedition against idolatry.

I t is believed that the few inhabitants remaining in Machu Picchu around 1540 fled quickly to avoid the risk of encountering the Spaniards. The invading troops had begun to penetrate the Vilcabamba region near the sanctuary, where the bulk of the Inca resistance had taken refuge. However, one has to search very carefully to find chronicles from that time that truly allow the history of the glory and the fall of this sacred place, and its subsequent slide into oblivion to be pieced together. *Quipu*, which take the place of a writing system and are composed of strands of cord containing various types of knots in multiple colors, are of no help. They remain largely undecipherable, and nothing pertaining to Machu Picchu has ever been decoded.

RELIGIOUS ZEAL

Peruvian historian Raúl Porras Barrenechea (1897–1960) lists Machu Picchu as a possible first objective of the evangelists' campaign to wipe out idolatry. They did not hesitate to use fire in the face of the minimal resistance, or in any place sacred to the Incas. He also specified that "burning out the Incas seemed to have been favored by the priests in the Vilcabamba area, a strategy that was secretly spread throughout Peru during the time Governor Lope García de Castro was in power, until 1565." During his explorations from 1911 to 1915, Hiram Bingham was struck by the numerous signs of ancient fires, something that was also noticed by other archaeologists in many of their excavations. But Machu Picchu was neither that lost or that forgotten: In a provision made in 1562 by the fourth viceroy of Peru, Count of Nieva (1510–1564), "Pijchu" is mentioned as part of a land division, entrusted first to Hernando Pizarro and then to Arias Maldonado. In May of 1565, the negotiator Diego Rodríguez de Figueroa, who traveled the Vilcabamba area working with the Inca rebels, spoke of "Picchu, which is in a peaceful area." The town of "Picho," as listed in manuscripts from 1568 found in the Departmental Archives of Cusco by Peruvian historians Luis Miguel Glave and María Isabel Remy, appears on a list of lands cultivated by the Incas in the Urubamba Valley, with the notation that it had been annexed and was controlled by Pachacuti.

FORGOTTEN TEMPLE
The stone temple cared for by the Intiwatana, in a photo taken during Hiram Bingham's 1912 expedition.

ABANDONED SITE
Vegetation grows from the sculpted stone in a place abandoned for centuries.

What Was the Treasure Found in Machu Picchu?

The material taken from Machu Picchu by Bingham is a mystery, one which can now be found at Yale University. Though researchers usually speak of some 5,000 artifacts, the Peruvian government recently demanded the return of more than 46,000 pieces. The confusion stems from the fact that many objects are comprised of numerous fragments. It is believed that only 350 of these pieces are suitable for display. The university agreed to return these objects (and an unspecified number of fragments) in an agreement reached in 2008, as long as a suitable museum is built in accordance with the specifications set forth by the university.

The Treasures of the Incas

Machu Picchu is a colossal testimony to the Incas' architectural abilities. Their ingenuity and skill, however, spill over into other forms of artistic expression: textiles, ceramics, goldsmithing, and ornaments made from other materials, which bear witness to their competence as artisans.

Textiles

Like other Andean cultures, the Incas were expert weavers, heirs of a tradition that began centuries earlier with the rise of the Cusco. To make garments, the Incas used horizontal and vertical looms with weaves composed of numerous threads, allowing them to make extremely detailed designs. They used llama, alpaca, and vicuña wool, the last being reserved exclusively for royalty. Alpacas can be up to 22 different colors, and exhibit the largest color range of any wool-producing animal. According to some researchers, *tocapu* (square designs with patterns in their center), such as those on the poncho to the right, could represent a rudimentary form of writing. The combination of blue and red (characteristic of royalty), as well as the scaled patterns around the neck, are clear indications that this garment belonged to a noble.

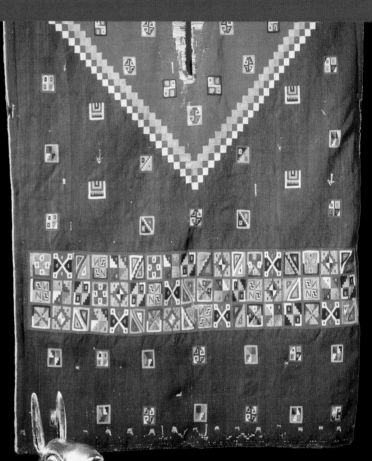

SILVER WORK
Alpaca worked in fine silver plate, next to a llama with a saddle decorated with geometric motifs. Camelids are one of the most often used motifs in Andean art.

CEREMONIAL VASES
Queros (the word means "wood," but they are also made of clay or metal) usually have geometric as well as figurative decorations.

Sacrificial Knives

Tumis are ceremonial knives that have a semicircular blade and a haft with a figure carved into it, usually a deity. These knives are found throughout the Andean range and were made by peoples prior to the Incas, such as the Sican culture. They are used in religious sacrifices, and there is evidence that they were also used in surgical procedures. They were usually made from a single sheet of metal.

SACRED PLANTS

Highly realistic representation of a corn plant, in silver, made to scale. Corn was a luxurious crop for the Incas, as the mountainous terrain of the Andes is not favorable for growing corn, and production was thus restricted to the valleys.

The Incas used this plant to make chicha, an alcoholic drink used in rituals which is still very popular in the Andes. Mills that were probably used to make chicha were found in Machu Picchu.

COLORED PLUMES

Numerous fabrics, ornaments and figurines were made using the beautiful feathers found in the Amazon region.

Alternative Hypotheses

Was Machu Picchu Built by the Atlanteans?

Accepting the Atlantean theory means ignoring the dates currently used by scientists, who estimate that Machu Picchu was built around 1450 CE, and dating its construction to a mythical time more than 2,000 years ago. Those who support this idea usually relate the destruction of the hypothetical continent of Atlantis directly with the appearance of the great Andean cultures. Thus, when Atlantis sank (because of a comet colliding with earth, according to some, or because of some nuclear force, according to others), the survivors fled to the Andes, where they built a new civilization similar to that which was destroyed.

Is the City Shaped Like an Animal, Like Cusco?

The Inca practice of reflecting aspects of nature in their works is well known by Andean archaeologists. In Machu Picchu, specific sacred rocks have been shaped to match the appearance of nearby mountains. The strongest example, however, is the design of the Inca capital, Cusco, whose layout recalls the figure of a puma. The practice of crafting buildings according to a natural or mythical model occurs in numerous ancient civilizations. Based on this knowledge, some authors, such as Fernando and Edgar Elorrieta Salazar, believe that Machu Picchu follows the same pattern, and they can see various animal figures in the citadel's structure: a reptile, a puma and a condor, according to the angle of sight and the area considered. This hypothesis, though it has not been accepted by the scientific community, is in line with the cosmic value of these animals in the Andean world (reptile = underworld, puma = earth, condor = sky).

IMAGINARY FIGURE?
Although it is difficult to distinguish the figure of a lizard or alligator in Machu Picchu's layout, if the outline is marked, it is almost impossible to miss.

Was Machu Picchu the Work of the Lemurians?

The Lemurian hypothesis is similar to that of Atlantis, though located on the continent of Lemuria, which was proposed by British zoologist Philip Sclater in the mid-19th century. He placed this continent in the Indian Ocean. Sclater used Lemuria as an attempt to explain the similarity between various species of animals endemic to Africa and India. With the arrival of the theories of plate tectonics and continental drift at the beginning of the 20th century, science ruled out this supposed lost continent. However, a plethora of spiritualists and members of the occult endowed Lemuria with a sense of the mythical and built the Lemurians into an extraordinary civilization that, when their continent sank, moved to the Andes, where they erected large monuments like Tiwanaku and Machu Picchu.

Were the First Inhabitants Jewish?

On September 21, 1823, far from Machu Picchu, in Manchester, New York, a young man named John Smith claimed to have received a visit from a messenger of God. This messenger introduced himself as Moroni and claimed to be the last of the prophets of the Nephite people. Later, Moroni took John Smith to a place where, hidden in the earth, Smith found a book written on sheets of gold, the *Book of Mormon*, the sacred text of the Mormons, who are also known as followers of the Church of the Latter-day Saints. This work consists of various books that tell of the unforeseen events experienced by the Jaredite and Lehi peoples who had traveled to America from Jerusalem between 2200 and 600 BCE. For the Mormons, and as indicated in some editions of the *Book of Mormon* bearing illustrations and photos to this effect, these Semitic peoples were involved in the construction of Machu Picchu. To support this claim, the Mormons consider the city, against all archaeological evidence, to be more than 2,000 years old.

ANCIENT CHRISTIANS
Bronze sculpture in the Mormon temple in Salt Lake City, Utah, showing various ethnic groups. The ancient Incas would have received the revelation of Christ in their time.

Were the Mines of King Solomon in Machu Picchu?

The theological debate over the origins of the mines of King Solomon, traditionally located (but never found) in the Biblical port of Ofir, began at the beginning of the 16th century, during the Age of Discovery, and it divided the Spaniards and the Portuguese, who were conquering and exploring the world. They each placed the mines in their new territories overseas. The country of Ofir was in vogue at that time as explorers sought to turn legends of treasure into palpable realities of gold and silver. The Solomon Islands, for example, were thus named because their discoverer, the Spaniard Álvaro de Mendaña, believed he had arrived at Ofir in 1568. According to some Spanish biblicists, the Mines of Solomon, whose riches had served to build and decorate the first temple in Jerusalem, were found in Inca Peru. This hypothesis was upheld by Spanish historian Fernando de Montesinos, from the 17th century, and by the Spaniard Benito Arias Montano (1527–1598), a priest, theologist, poet, and librarian in the El Escorial Monastery who was detained (and absolved) by the Holy Inquisition.

How were the Stone Blocks Put Together?

Although how the Andean peoples polished the stones is known, the Incas themselves retained oral traditions of a supernatural nature. One of these stories talks about the bird Kak'aqllu, who knew a way to soften rocks, and thus shaped them more easily. An Inca god, according to the legend, ripped out its tongue to keep him from revealing the secret. Another traditional story tells that the ever-wise Incas knew of a preparation called *ayaconchi*, made from the juices of certain mysterious plants, which could soften rocks so they could be shaped more easily. Some people consider this story to be true, and have created hypotheses about which plants in the Andean region might have this quality.

BIBLICAL GOLD
Engraving by Gustave Doré representing King Solomon. Some hypotheses indicate that the source of the biblical king's riches was in Inca territory.

Was the City Built by Extra-terrestrials?

In 1983, actress and New Age advocate Shirley MacLaine published *Out on a Limb*, an autobiographical book describing her spiritual awakening, the result of her travels to various sacred places around the world, including Machu Picchu. Three years later, the actress could be found in Cusco, working on a mini-series based on her book. Filming did not proceed without delays, and one of the most significant was caused by Peru's National Cultural Institute, which demanded that the team remove eight pages from the script in which they asserted that Machu Picchu had been built by extraterrestrials. This was no obstacle to Shirley MacLaine, who, once filming had finished and she had returned home, publicly stated to whomever wanted to listen: "I know that I was an Inca priestess."

POWER OF THE ORIENT
Illustration from the 19th century showing emperor Kublai Khan on an elephant. It has been suggested that he is the ancestor of the ancient Inca lords.

Is the Origin of the Incas in China?

British explorer Clements R. Markham (1830–1916) echoed the Asian factor in *Cuzco: a Journey to the Ancient Capital of Peru* (1856). He first cites German poet Friedrich von Schlegel (1772–1829), who in his *Aesthetic and Miscellaneous Works* states: "The founders of the Kingdom of Peru emigrated from eastern China and the Indian islands." He then makes a comparison to naturalist Alexander von Humboldt, who shared the same hypothesis. Finally, he mentions naturalist Mariano Rivero, who wrote in *Peruvian Antiquities* (1841): "There is no doubt that Bochica (the civilizing god of the ChiBCEha people of Colombia) and Manco Cápac were Buddhist priests who, by their superior doctrine, managed to rule the souls of the indigenous peoples."

Did the Incas Descend from Genghis Khan?

British writer John Ranking proposed in 1827 that Manco Cápac was the son of Mongolian emperor Kublai Khan, grandson of Genghis Khan. He published this theory in a book with an almost interminable title: *Historical Researches on the Conquest of Peru, Mexico, Bogota, Natchez, and Talomeco in the Thirteenth Century by the Mongols, Accompanied by Elephants: and the Local Agreement of History and Tradition with the Remains of Elephants and Mastodons Found in the New World.*

To See and Visit

▼ OTHER PLACES OF INTEREST

CITY OF CUSCO
PERU

The ancient Inca capital is 80 miles from Machu Picchu, and is the traditional point of departure for tourists visiting the ruins. In Cusco, you can visit the Museum of Pre-Columbian Art, the Coricancha Temple Museum (Temple of the Sun), and the current Plaza de Armas, an ancient Incan ceremonial site.

PÍSAC
PERU

This city is located 20 miles from Cusco, to the east of Vilcabamba. This is one of the end points of the Sacred Valley of the Incas, Ollantaytambo being the other. The city also has a busy market and an astronomical observatory.

OLLANTAYTAMBO
PERU

Located 19 miles east of Machu Picchu, this city was the residence of Pachacuti, and was later the center of the resistance led by Manco Inca Yupanqui. The train from Cusco to Machu Picchu travels through the city.

VILCABAMBA
PERU

Vilcabamba was the Incas' last refuge. It was conquered in 1572, when the last Inca, Túpac Amaru I, was executed. Located some 30 miles west of Machu Picchu, today the city is called Espíritu Pampa (Spirit of the Plain – The name Vilcabamba means "sacred plain.") The ruins are divided into four sectors, and have been excavated in recent years by numerous archaeologists.

Machu Picchu

HOW TO GET THERE

The ruins can be visited any day of the year. Most visitors travel to Machu Picchu by plane, via Lima, with a domestic flight to Cusco. From there, a train takes the visitor to Aguas Calientes, also known as Machu-Picchu Pueblo, and it's a short half-hour by bus to the archaeological site via Hiram Bingham Highway. The Manuel Chávez Ballón Museum is right next to Ruins Bridge and holds some 200 stone, metal, and ceramic objects from the Inca culture.

PROTECTED AREA

Machu Picchu was declared a UNESCO World Heritage Site for both its cultural and natural wealth, thanks to the biological diversity found in the area. The protected area, 32,000 hectares, contains an abundance of flora, including numerous species of orchids, and several unique species of fauna, such as the giant hummingbird (the largest in the world), the spectacled bear (the only bear in South America), and the Andean cock-of-the-rock, the national bird of Peru.

SEASON

As the most-visited tourist destination in Peru (it receives almost a half-million visitors per year), Machu Picchu can be crowded in the high season. Additionally, its location (surrounded by the Urubamba River, at the top of the mountain) makes it wise to choose one's trip date carefully. Visiting during the rainy season (December to April) is not recommended, and June and July are the coldest months there.

Inca Trail

Those who wish to immerse themselves fully in the Andes and the Inca world can travel to Machu Picchu on foot, following part of the road built by the Incas between Machu Picchu and Cusco. The trail is 30 miles long, and it takes two to four days to walk it. Along the Inca Trail one finds numerous archaeological sites (such as Llaqtapata, Huayllabamba, or Runkuraqay), in addition to an extraordinary and changing landscape that ranges from the high mountains to the plains.

CHOQUEQUIRAO
PERU

Choquequirao is considered Machu Picchu's sister city, being similar in architecture and layout. It's name means "cradle of gold," and it is 20 miles southwest of Machu Picchu. Although it cannot compete with Machu Picchu, it has the advantage of being less crowded. A two day journey on foot is required to access the site.

CHINCHERO
PERU

Chinchero is located 17 miles from Cusco and was at one time the royal palace of Túpac Inca Yupanqui, Pachacuti's son and successor. The current inhabitants built their homes on top of the Inca ruins. The Sunday market and the church are the major tourist attractions.

LLAQTAPATA
PERU

Also called Patallacta, this city is found 2.5 miles west of Machu Picchu. It was burned by Manco Inca Yupanqui when he retreated to Vilcabamba so that the Spaniards could not find it.

PEABODY MUSEUM OF ARCHAEOLOGY
CAMBRIDGE, MASS.

This museum houses the treasures taken from Peru on loan by Hiram Bingham during his expeditions. Despite requests made by Bingham, the National Geographic Society, and, later, the Peruvian government, the museum has yet to return the objects and continues to display them. Today, steps are being taken to return the objects to Peru.

Connecting Heaven and Earth

Stonehenge is one of the greatest mysteries of the Ancient World. Ever since dealers in ancient things said that it was a druid temple four centuries ago, the theories have multiplied. An astronomical computer, a mathematical calendar, a focal point of terrestrial energies and a healing center are just some of the ideas that have been passed around in recent years. Which of these are viable, and which are merely imaginative interpretations?

This monumental complex was built by a society in the Stone Age. How did these ancient people build such a sophisticated structure using only primitive technologies? The sarsen sandstone blocks, which weigh up to 35 metric tons, were transported 19 miles to the site. Even more extraordinary are the "bluestones" (blocks of blue sandstone weighing between 4 and 8 metric tons) from the Preseli hills, some 155 miles away.

Thanks to modern archaeology, we know something about the era in which Stonehenge was built. Experts have agreed on a general chronology: construction began between 3000 and 2920 BCE (Phase 1), with a circular enclosure and a circle of small pits, known as the "Aubrey Holes," which possibly once contained bluestones. Afterward, they erected wooden posts. The location was also, from its creation until around 2400 BCE, a burial ground for cremated human remains. At some point, in the period from 2620 to 2480 BCE (Phase 2), the Welsh bluestones were placed in a circle around the horseshoe, a formation of five trilithons enclosed within a circle of 30 blocks of sarsen. It is believed that around these dates, other stones were also erected in the entrance area (the "Slaughter Stone" and the "Heel Stone") and outside the main complex (the "Station Stones"). The axis of Stonehenge aligns with the setting sun on the winter solstice and with the rising sun on the summer solstice.

Three additional stages of construction have been identified. During Phase 3 (2480 to 2280 BCE) a new circle of bluestones were raised in the center of Stonehenge, built with stones from Bluestonehenge, which used to be located next to the River Avon but was taken down. During this period Stonehenge and Bluestonehenge were connected by a road known as "The Avenue." During Phase 4 (2270 to 2020 BCE), the bluestones were redistributed and during Phase 5 (2020 to 1520 BCE) some were sculpted.

In recent years, new excavations have helped us to understand Stonehenge in context – and in archaeology, context is everything – with the discovery of an enormous settlement buried underneath the great Durrington Walls enclosure, just 2 miles away. Together with Bluestonehenge, this fact demonstrates that Stonehenge was not constructed as an isolated site, but it was part of a larger complex of stones and wooden circles, with the two centers connected by the River Avon. While Stonehenge was the domain of the dead, the wooden circles of Durrington Walls were the place where the living celebrated the solstices. Their builders were ancient British peoples, whose ancestors were a mixture of indigenous hunters and agricultural immigrants.

In 2008, the reason why Stonehenge had this specific relationship with the solstices was discovered. Part of "The Avenue" was excavated which leads from Stonehenge along the axis of the solstice and it was found that its ridges and trenches follow a series of natural hills which are aligned with the solstice. The prehistoric men observed this incidental alignment in the natural landscape, and later embellished it with ridges and trenches.

Maybe Stonehenge was built to mark this "axis mundi," where the Earth and the Heavens meet.

Mike Parker Pearson

Professor of Archaeology at Sheffield University, UK. He published 14 books and more than 100 papers dedicated to the prehistory of northern Europe. He is considered one of the major experts on Stonehenge.

LIGHTS
It is at dawn, especially during the solstices, that the lighting takes on that magical sense that characterizes Stonehenge.

Stonehenge: Neolithic Remains

Visited by thousands every year, this megalithic monument was deemed by some studies an astronomical observatory, and by others a temple for worshiping the dead. The mystery remains.

Now, in the twenty-first century, the era of the Internet, particle acceleration and 3D cinema, humans remain fascinated by the enigmas of our distant past.

What is it about the first human constructions, crude blocks of stone placed on the ground in primal geometric forms, that generates so much interest, including from people not especially interested in archaeology, history or art?

In the Neolithic Age, the final stage of prehistory, during which man began agriculture and animal husbandry, Atlantic Europe, and especially the British Isles, were filled with simple constructions called *cromlechs*, consisting of a series of *menhirs* or large vertical stones that form circles or ellipses. Amongst the more than one thousand cromlechs found in Great Britain and Ireland, the most well-known are Callanish and Brodgar in Scotland, and Castlerigg, Long Meg, Avebury and Stonehenge in England. While similar in some ways, notable differences exist between them. Avebury, near to Stonehenge, is so large –1099 feet in diameter – that it is hard to see its circular shape from the ground. Meanwhile Callanish, whose biggest stones are 16 feet tall, only measures 42 feet in diameter.

The most unique of all the prehistoric monuments is, without doubt, Stonehenge. It is located in the south of England, some 86 miles west of London. It does not stand out due to its size –the outer circle only measures 98 feet in diameter – but rather due to its complexity and to its role as part of an extensive assembly of ancient ruins. As a matter of fact, the complexity of Stonehenge led the archaeologists to distinguish between the circles of stones and what they came to call "henges," a name taken from the Stonehenge site itself and which designates complexes of prehistoric origin made up of a circular embankment with concentric areas in the middle which are used for gravestones and/or structures of stone or wood.

To understand Stonehenge, we must take a step back from the touristic viewpoint, which focuses on the artistic design – the circle of stones raised in the final phase of its construction – and overlooks the archaeological aspect and five centuries of work.

A map or aerial image of the area allows us to see that Stonehenge includes

MILESTONE
Stonehenge is a masterpiece of engineering. The 30 giant stones that formed the outer circle —17 of which still remain in place— weigh 50 metric tons each.

in addition to the famous monoliths: a trench, an embankment, and a circle of small holes – all concentric – as well as various gravestones, isolated single monoliths as well as many other ancient remains in its surroundings.

But in an area of 2.5 acres, the equivalent of a soccer field, the great diversity of neolithic remains is not even the most impressive aspect of Stonehenge nor what has made this megalithic monument the most visited prehistoric site in the world for years.

ARCHITECTURAL FEAT

A brief comparison of Stonehenge with any of the other stone circles cited shows a fundamental difference: while the other circles of Great Britain and Europe are formed by unpolished monoliths, raised as they were found, the menhirs of Stonehenge were polished to give them an orthogonal shape (with straight angles) to make them capable of holding up other megaliths as lintels. The ability shown in this design puts the builders of Stonehenge on a much higher level than the creators of Callanish, Brodgar or Castlerigg, for example.

To justly evaluate the feats of the Stonehenge architects, we place the work in the context of its location and time period. In any era, the evolution of the historic periods present notable geographic differences. For example around 3000 BCE – the beginning phase of Stonehenge – while the cultures of Mesopotamia had already entered the Bronze Age, the men of the European Atlantic were still in the Stone Age. This is the cause of certain anachronisms that today seem to clash: the Sumerians of Uruk, in Mesopotamia, invented the wheel and introduced writing between 3500 and 3300 BCE. Various centuries later, the builders of Stonehenge would have found the transportation of the monoliths to be much easier with the help of a set of wheels. But these things took another few centuries to arrive in Great Britain.

The chronological misalignment between the advanced cultures of the Near East and the then outlying Europe is even more evident in the face of the discovery that the initial circles of Stonehenge are contemporaries of the Giza pyramids. Alongside such complex architecture, the British stone circles don't begin to compare. This inferiority in comparison with the monuments of one of the greatest civilizations of history does not in any way minimize the construction feats of the population of southwest Britain 5000 years ago. Especially when we take into account the details that can go unnoticed by the uninitiated upon first examination of the monument: the stones utilized are not native to the area, and were cleverly carved to the degree that would be expected of a carpenter, rather than that of a stone-cutter.

Effectively, none of the types of stone found in Stonehenge are native to the area: the blocks of bluestone (igneous rocks, mainly doleritic) which are up to 6.5 feet high and weigh 4 metric tons, come from mountains 150 miles away as the crow flies; whilst the monoliths of silica sandstone, some of which are over 23 feet tall and weigh 40 metric tons were transported from a site 18 miles away. Stonehenge was built in various phases, starting with using horses between the Neolithic Age and the beginning of the European Bronze Age. According to the most recent studies, the first undertaking was some

▲

CELEBRATION
More than 30,000 people come together each year at Stonehenge to celebrate the solstices. With dance, drums, food and pagan rituals, they welcome the arrival of the warm weather.

▼

THE AVENUE
A processional path 75 feet wide and 2 miles long cuts through the trench of 341 feet in diameter that surrounds Stonehenge. It is known as "The Avenue" and reaches the River Avon.

5000 years ago, around 3000 BCE, when the population of the plains to the southwest of Great Britain built the embankment and the circular ditch of 378 feet in diameter and dug 56 holes within that circle – known as the "Aubrey Holes" – that likely held the bluestones brought, for reasons unknown, from the Preseli mountains, situated in southwest Wales. In the following centuries, this circular area with two entrances seems to have been filled with more complex wooden structures that possibly served to

give relevance to the funeral ceremonies that were practiced in the area. Four to five centuries later, around 2600 or 2500 BCE, the builders of Stonehenge raised the monoliths of silica sandstone, at the same time as they decided to reseat the bluestones.

THE BLUESTONES
Today, this circle of bluestones, some of which are nearly 6.5 feet high and weigh 4 metric tons, are eclipsed by the long shadow of the silica sandstone monoliths–also known as

Continued on page 60 ▶

Precocious Astronomers?

An emblem of European architecture from the Bronze Age, this complex is a masterpiece of an ancient society interested in the observation of the stars. They began a difficult transition from the traditional life of hunting to the arduous labor of agricultural life.

The Astronomical Calendar

Stonehenge was a temple for the observation of astronomical phenomena, a calendar that permitted foretelling of the arrival of the seasons and thus guided the activities of the peasants and livestock farmers.

THE STRUCTURE

Stonehenge is made up of concentric circles of megaliths of up to 16 ft high. Perfectly placed in the ground, they can calculate the movement of the sun and the moon and indicate the solstices and eclipses.

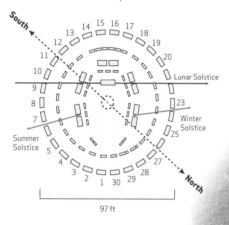

97 ft

Solstices

Times in the year during which the sun reaches its zenith in the tropics. The summer solstice is the longest day of the year, the winter solstice, the shortest.

From the Neolithic to the Bronze Age

Every 18,6 years the moon reaches an extreme azimuth on the horizon, the "lunar standstill." In Stonehenge the moon lines up over the sun, reflecting the yearning in the age of hunters that attributed symbolism to the blue heavenly body.

----- Path of the Sun
----- Path of the Moon

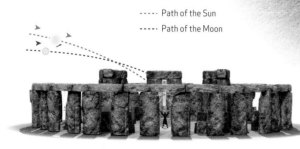

The Stones

They are known as "sarsen" (siliceous sandstone). The lintels weigh up to 7 metric tons and the pillars 25 metric tons.

SECOND RING

THIRD RING

Slaughter Stone

enigmas

Who Else Collaborated with the Ancient Britons in the Construction of Stonehenge?

During one of the archaeological excavations carried out in the area where Stonehenge was erected, the team headed by English professor Richard Atkinson found a dagger made of stone whose carved edge was very similar to the daggers from the Greek civilization that flourished in Mycenae in 1500 BCE. That discovery caused them to surmise that the Mycenaeans may have been involved in the construction of the monument, something that was later discarded.

TRILITHONS
These consist of two pillars of stone crowned by a lintel 14.5 ft above the ground.

FOURTH RING

CROMLECH
A structure with a horseshoe shape made of 19 menhirs, each 10 ft high.

MONOLITHS
Known as menhirs, they are vertical blocks of stone.

FIRST RING

An Ancient Construction

Stonehenge represents a colossal effort of planning and execution. The monument took on diverse forms over 40 generations of existence.

1 MOVING THE STONES
The stones were brought from the surrounding areas. It is possible that the menhirs brought from Wales were transported by rafts on the River Avon.

2 POSITIONING
On the platform, a circular pit was dug, and the stones were pushed in using levers and tree trunks.

3 THE MENHIRS
Once the megaliths were in the pit, they were placed upright using ropes and supports, and set into the ground.

4 PLACEMENT OF THE LINTELS
The lintels were raised using a tower of tree trunks. The stones had chiseled cavities and protrusions to ensure a perfect fit.

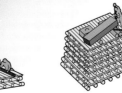

sarsen stones–raised around them many decades later. These are 30 monoliths of up to 23 feet tall, weighing 40 metric tons, carved into orthogonal shapes and joined at the top by lintels, forming a compact circle. Today, only half of the sarsen stones remain standing. Inside these two distinctive circles of stone is a final structure, this time in the shape of a horseshoe. It is made up of five trilithons of silica sandstone, is open toward the northeast, and flanked by an internal line of smaller bluestones facing in the same direction: toward the daybreak of the summer solstice. Between 2480 BCE and 2280 BCE an avenue 2 miles long was built. It reached the River Avon and formed part of the disjointed assembly of prehistoric remains found around Stonehenge. These nearby remains include the Cursus (a wide, almost straight road 2 miles long), the Woodhenge Circles (similar to Stonehenge but made of wood) and Durrington Walls. The latter is an enormous circular terrace that contains two further circles and around which remains of a Neolithic population were found. The discovery of Woodhenge, at the beginning of the twentieth century, was important to the archaeological research exploring the evolution of Stonehenge. The remains of the woodwork indicate that, before erecting the stone structure, the constructors had built a base of tree trunks that remained in place for multiple centuries. This explains why, when they decided to substitute stone for wood, they treated the stone as if they were carpenters. Instead of joining the jambs and lintels with mortar, or stacking them in the rudimentary dry stone method, they used dovetail joints–a technique carpenters call "mortise and tenon" – which holds together the monoliths with precision, strength,

and reliability. That half of the structure has remained standing for 4500 years, in an extremely windy, humid, and cold area, demonstrates the great ability of the carpenters who worked the stone. The location of Stonehenge allows the monument to be seen from a distance of 1.25 miles from almost all angles. Its alignment with the rising sun in the summer solstice and with the sunset in the winter solstice fed the hypothesis for many years that it was an astronomical observatory and a place for worshiping deities associated with natural astronomy. As a matter of fact, the neighboring circles of Woodhenge and Durrington Walls also have alignments that coincide with the solstices.

These precise placements and orientations, combined with the evocative landscape and the antiquity of the site, mean that every June 21, since the '70s, Stonehenge has had an irresistible pull for hippies, pagan sects, druids and astrology aficionados, who camp in its surroundings (now under the watchful eye of "bobbies" and the English Heritage functionaries) to celebrate the first dawn of summer. Recent research by archaeologists suggests, however, that the original purpose of Stonehenge was not related to astronomy but rather to the worship of the dead, although no doubt the builders knew much about the pathways of the sun through the sky and used them as reference points for building the monument. Generation after generation, Stonehenge arouses curiosity, both among those that have had the opportunity to visit its venerable monoliths, and for experts who work on the unsolvable enigmas, analyzing the site inch by inch; and not only the stones, but all the remains, near and far, left by the men who lived in the region 5000 years ago.

Gerald Hawkins
1928–2003

English astronomer who became famous in the '70s when he published a study about Stonehenge in which he claimed the Neolithic construction was an astronomical calendar. This work, titled *Stonehenge Decoded*, was published by the magazine *Nature* in 1963, and an edited version appeared in a book of the same name two years later. Hawkins carried out his work by entering the positions of the great stones and other characteristics of Stonehenge into a primitive IBM 7090 computer and using the data obtained to model the movements of the sun and moon. Thanks to this study, Hawkings is today considered one of the fathers of archeoastronomy.

THEORY With a doctorate in radioastronomy, Hawkins claimed Stonehenge was a "Neolithic computer" that, amongst other things, served to predict eclipses.

Stuart Piggott
1910–1996

This British professor, a specialist in Celtic culture, actively participated in the excavations done in the middle of the last century. This venture discovered engravings made with hatchets, clubs and daggers on the sarsen stones in the areas around Stonehenge.

NEOLITHIC The contributions of Piggott to archaeology were linked with this prehistoric age.

◀ *Continued from page 57*

M. Parker Pearson

English archaeologist from the University of Sheffield who dedicated years of his work to Stonehenge. Leading a team of his colleagues and countrymen, he discovered the site called "Bluehenge" (or "Bluestonehenge") named for the color of the 27 stones placed in the area. Mike Parker Pearson was part of the Stonehenge Riverside Project, financed by the National Geographic Society and the UK Arts and Humanities Research Council, with the support of the English Heritage. During this project it was discovered that the area where the megalithic structure stands functioned as a cemetery for more than 500 years. Members of the ancient British royal family and their descendants were buried there. It also highlighted the significance of the River Avon which: "formed a channel between the living and the dead. According to the beliefs of the time, people left the land of the living at the river and entered the land of the dead in Stonehenge."

CONNECTION According to Parker Pearson, Durrington Walls represents the land of the living and Stonehenge the domain of their dead ancestors. The two sites were linked by seasonal processions that followed a trajectory indicated by the paths and the river.

"I don't believe that ordinary people were buried at Stonehenge. It was a special place in that period. Anyone buried there must have had good credentials." M. P. P.

Richard C. Atkinson

1920–1994

British archaeologist who worked in close collaboration with Stuart Piggott and formed his own theory about the construction of Stonehenge. He directed a series of excavations in the area between 1950 and 1964. Unfortunately he did not keep a suitable record of this work, and his discoveries remained unknown for years. After Atkinson's death, some archaeological pieces obtained in his excavations and more than 2000 photographs taken in the area were found in his home.

CALCULATION According to Professor Atkinson, the transportation of each stone that forms part of Stonehenge required the efforts of 1500 men and took at least seven weeks.

Prehistoric Architecture

The megalithic structure was erected on Salisbury Plain, in the south of England. Its design combines stone, wood and earth. It was finalized over a period of more than 1,400 years and, according to the experts, it is one of the most important prehistoric constructions in Europe.

The Evolution of Prehistoric Architecture

The megalithic ruins are located some 80 miles west of London, the result of the architectural evolution of prehistory. While it is unclear today why they were built, we are certain of their astronomical efficiency and of their use as a burial sanctuary.

GREAT CURSUS

2 miles of channeled road. This was built around 3500 BCE. Its purpose is unknown.

STONEHENGE

After the Great Cursus, a construction technique was developed that converted it into one of the most architecturally advanced works of the period.

THE AVENUE

The journey that symbolized the passing from life to death continued on the cobbled avenue after coming down the River Avon from Durrington Walls.

1 2950-2900 BCE

In the middle of the Neolithic Age, the embankment was prepared and the circular trench was dug. Directly inside the earthen bank is what is known as the "Aubrey Circle."

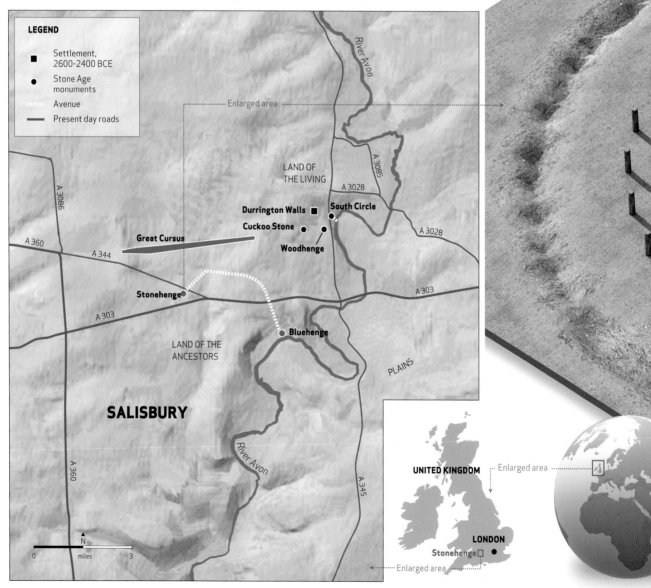

LEGEND

- ■ Settlement, 2600-2400 BCE
- ● Stone Age monuments
- ▦▦▦ Avenue
- —— Present day roads

River Avon

Enlarged area

LAND OF THE LIVING

A 3085

A 3028

Durrington Walls ■ ●**South Circle**

Cuckoo Stone ●

A 3028

Great Cursus

A 3086

A 360

A 344

Woodhenge ●

A 303

Stonehenge ●

A 303

Bluehenge ●

LAND OF THE ANCESTORS

PLAINS

SALISBURY

A 360

River Avon

A 345

N

0   miles   3

UNITED KINGDOM   Enlarged area

LONDON
Stonehenge □   ●

Enlarged area

Could it Have Been a Healing Sanctuary?

Astrological observatory, religious temple, fertility temple...We aren't short of theories to explain the origin of Stonehenge, and in 2008 the British archaeologist Tim Darvill risked yet another: after finding various bones with different injuries during an excavation sponsored by the BBCE, he suggested that it could have been a place where pilgrims traveled in order to cure their sicknesses, something like a "Neolithic Lourdes."

enigmas

Phases of Construction

The historian and archaeologist Richard Atkinson directed the excavation of Stonehenge during 1940-1964. He concluded that the monument was built in three essential phases.

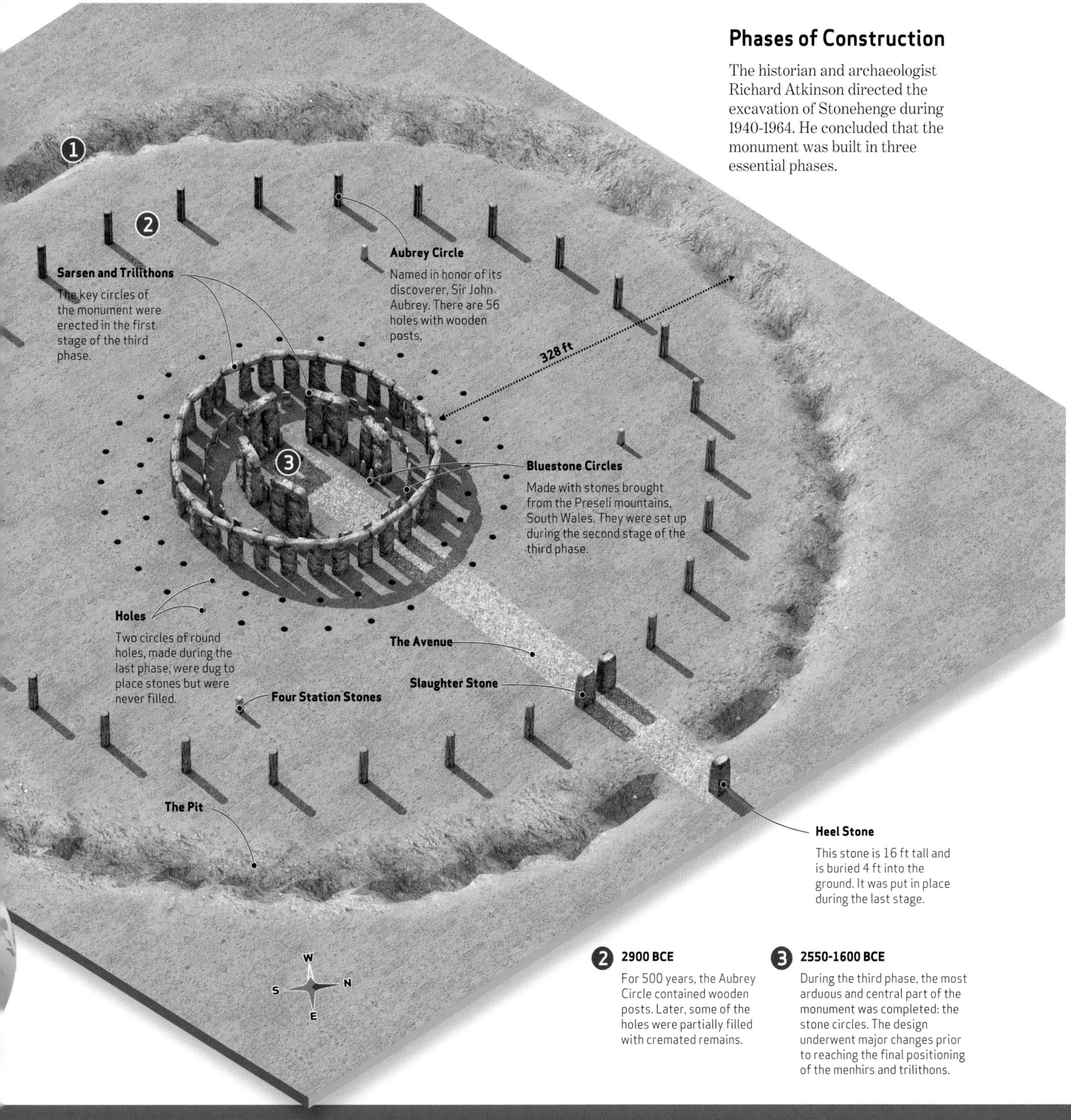

① ②

Sarsen and Trilithons

The key circles of the monument were erected in the first stage of the third phase.

Aubrey Circle

Named in honor of its discoverer, Sir John Aubrey. There are 56 holes with wooden posts.

328 ft

③

Bluestone Circles

Made with stones brought from the Preseli mountains, South Wales. They were set up during the second stage of the third phase.

Holes

Two circles of round holes, made during the last phase, were dug to place stones but were never filled.

The Avenue

Slaughter Stone

Four Station Stones

The Pit

Heel Stone

This stone is 16 ft tall and is buried 4 ft into the ground. It was put in place during the last stage.

W · N · S · E

② 2900 BCE

For 500 years, the Aubrey Circle contained wooden posts. Later, some of the holes were partially filled with cremated remains.

③ 2550-1600 BCE

During the third phase, the most arduous and central part of the monument was completed: the stone circles. The design underwent major changes prior to reaching the final positioning of the menhirs and trilithons.

A Millennium of Work

Recent studies have shown that the construction of Stonehenge required about a thousand years of collective work. According to the most convincing hypotheses thus far, they were built in connection with the development of religious rituals and astronomical observation, to which the priestly elite were devoted.

The Heel Stone

The circle is the dominant figure at Stonehenge. The north-eastern side of the monument opens up into a wide "avenue" which at some point appears to have been the main entrance to the henge. And at the opposite side from the avenue, and outside of the circle, a solitary monolith was erected, which was named the Heel Stone due to its conical shape.

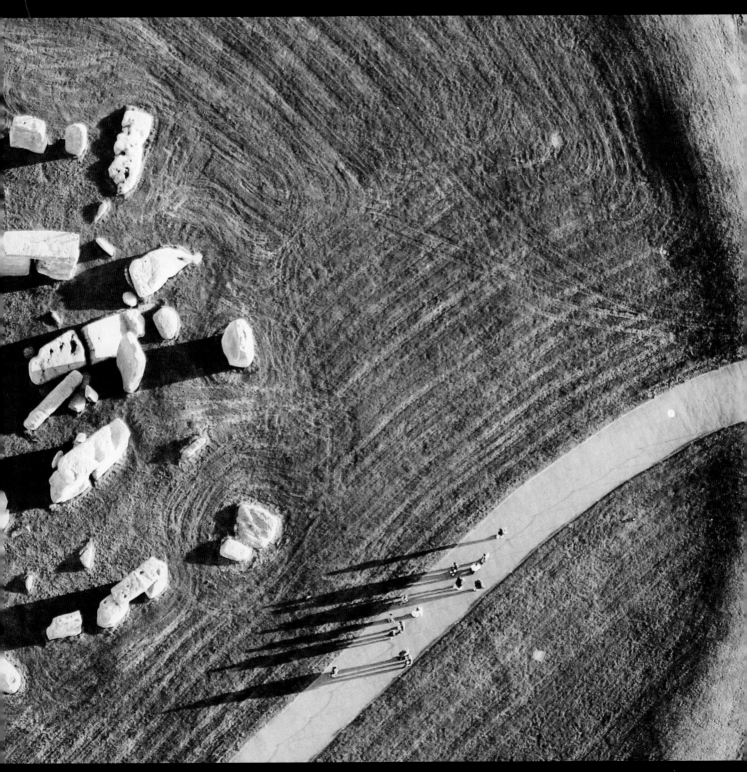

TECHNIQUE The arches and circular shapes at Stonehenge reveal the builders' advanced mastery of geometry.

How Did the Stones Get to Stonehenge?

While Stonehenge is mostly associated with the siliceous sandstone monoliths that were expertly carved in order to support lintels of the same size, the smaller blocks, called "bluestones," are the most mysterious.

The chemical analysis of the almost eighty bluestones which can be found today at Stonehenge showed that they came from the Preseli Hills, situated in southeast Wales. The tests were so precise that it was possible to locate their origin in an area called Carn Menyn. They were slabs of schist and dolerite – dark-colored and fine-textured igneous rocks – which form spectacular pinnacles, and were probably revered by the people of the era. These rocks are white or cream in color, but they are called "bluestones" because they turn blue when wet by the rain.

Thanks to the natural configuration of these pinnacles, the designers of Stonehenge only had to chip away at them from the base to separate them from the rock face. The most common question,

of course, is: How did they transport them? According to the most advanced studies, the most logical route, of around 249 miles, would have included the transportation of several dozen blocks of around four tons each, and the employment of wooden platforms over greased guides, to the waters of the East Cleddau river. Rafts made out of tree trunks would have been used to navigate the Daugleddau estuary, the Atlantic coast of the Bristol channel, and the River Avon, near Avon county (not the same river as the one near Stonehenge, though it has the same name). Then, they would have had to travel by land again to arrive at Stonehenge.

They completed the entire route dragging the heavy blocks and using only human manpower. We know this because in Great Britain in 2500 BCE, pack animals were not yet domesticated.

A COMPLICATED ROUTE

The intricate route required some level of diplomacy: the porters had to cross the lands of other clans. They also would have needed a good sense of direction and a detailed knowledge of the geography of the area since the route involved constant changes of direction and included various transitional journeys between nearby waterways. It is not known whether these nearly eighty blocks were carried during one trip: this strategy would have involved hundreds of young and able-bodied men from the region leaving their homes, crops, cattle and hunting. Additionally, they may have had to leave their clans defenseless in order to take part in the venture. This leads to the theory that most likely the bluestone blocks were hauled to the site over a period of several years.

Bluehenge, the Last Great Enigma

One of the most recent and interesting discoveries in the surroundings of the great English megalithic monument was a henge 82 feet in diameter, which housed a stone circle and which was located at the point where Stonehenge's processional avenue reached the River Avon, 1 mile to the southwest of the burial monument.

This newly found circle revealed a significant fact: the remains of bluestones were found inside it, like those brought from the Preseli Hills to build Stonehenge. For this reason, the archaeologists named it Bluehenge (or, some call it Bluestonehenge).

It is suspected that around twenty-five of the bluestones that ended up at Stonehenge were previously in this circle, based on a series of holes that were also found at this site. Later research additionally suggested that Bluehenge could have been the site where the bodies were cremated after being transported downriver from Durrington Walls village and before being buried at Stonehenge.

How Was the Complex Built?

Breaking with the traditional perception of crudeness and primitivism which distorts the image of prehistoric man, the builders of Stonehenge employed original and advanced methods for their time in Neolithic Europe.

Nearly all of the stone circles are made of unpolished monoliths. The bluestones used in the first phases of Stonehenge's construction were placed just as they were mined from the ground. The notable exception to this rule are the siliceous sandstone monoliths from the last phases of construction, which are carefully smoothed down to an almost orthogonal shape, apt for forming part of a much more complex construction. Effectively, the builders of the final phase of Stonehenge took an enormous step forward in the design of this type of monument when they designed structures with lintels. While the latest research suggests that the bluestone circle could have also been covered by lintels, this hypothesis has not been tested and no vestiges of this possibility remain. Half of the linteled structures made out of silica sandstone have lasted 4,500 years, which highlights the great ability of this last generation of builders during the transition between the Neolithic period and the British Bronze Age. Silica sandstone is a sedimentary rock widely used in construction. It is possible to shape it with tools made of the same stone, but this is an arduous task, because it splits into tiny pieces. Study of the monoliths indicates that various people worked their surface.

SURPRISING TECHNIQUES

The results of all of this effort are impressive. Although, as is logical, the construction did not reach the level of perfection of the walls built in later periods, the blocks of sandstone at Stonehenge come reasonably close to that which a Roman or medieval stonemason might call an "ashlar," which is to say, a stone carved until it forms the shape of a cuboid rectangle. The monoliths which are vertically positioned even have a certain entasis, a widening in the middle area, which is a primitive imitation of what the Greeks did with their temple columns, adding a slight convex curve to correct the visual illusion of concavity produced by a straight shaft. But the most surprising thing about the Stonehenge construction is the use of the dovetail technique used to put the blocks into place without using mortar: the lintels fit into each other and to the monoliths that support them through the articulation of concave shapes with convex shapes, an intermeshing that is not visible and was only discovered after a detailed examination of the fallen pieces.

How Did They Mount the Stones?

A recent experiment has demonstrated that a group of approximately 150 people can lift a monolith of a weight and size similar to the largest of those at Stonehenge (some 25 metric tons). Today it is thought that this is the approximate amount of people who worked on the erecting procedure. A few decades ago, it was thought that the British people of the Neolithic period were not capable of making structures of this type, but if it is true that they were able to transport enormous stones hundreds of miles, wouldn't they have known about the benefits of a complex lever system? The British archaeologist Richard Atkinson asked himself this question. He talked about the three phases of Stonehenge's construction. The first was between 2950 and 2900 BCE, when they made the embankment and the circular trench; the next in 2900 BCE, when they erected some 80 blocks of blue sandstone, arranged in the shape of a horseshoe; and the last one was between 2550 and 1600 BCE, when the bluestones were moved into their current positions on the inside of the circle. This was also when they moved the Slaughter Stone opposite the trilithons brought from the south of Wales. According to Atkinson, Stonehenge was abandoned around 1100 BCE, and left in a similar condition to that in which it is found today.

FUNCTIONAL CARVING
The stones were ingeniously carved into matching protrusions and cavities to make a perfect joint between columns and lintels.

RECONSTRUCTION
A group of archaeologists reproduced the mechanisms for the transportation of the monoliths in Gloucestershire.

What Was the Purpose of Stonehenge?

Why was Stonehenge really built? While in recent years a good quantity of hypotheses have been rejected, many of them corrupted by legends and traditions, the answer is still far from conclusive.

Outside of England, Stonehenge became immensely popular in the 1970s, when the hippie movement made it a symbol of spirituality and communion with nature. On the island, however, there are more than a hundred generations of locals who have asked themselves what the stones lying in a circle in the plains of Salisbury were placed there for. During more than 30 centuries (Stonehenge was abandoned around 1500 BCE) the inhabitants of southeast England, as well as foreigners, came up with a thousand stories, some far-fetched and others based on the historical and archaeological knowledge of each period.

Among the few foreigners interested in Stonehenge in ancient times was the Sicilian historian of Greek origin, Diodorus Siculus, who lived in the first century BCE, and thought the stone circle was a monument dedicated to Apollo. During this time, Britain had not yet been colonized by Rome, and so this reference to the Greek-Roman god could be understood as the historian taking license to clarify to his readers what he meant. The commentary, however, does not give many clues about the function of Stonehenge, seeing as Apollo is the God of the sun, but also the god of healing, prophecy, beauty and art.

During the Middle Ages, the monument was linked with the magical activities of Merlin, the Welsh magician of the legendary King Arthur, and it was believed that the stones came from Ireland. In the Early Modern Period, the first attempts to bring interest in Stonehenge into a more scientific realm conflicted with the older obscurantist traditions – in the seventeenth century it was still said that whoever tried to count the stones of the monument would die. In the eighteenth century, the antique dealer William Stukeley contributed some of the first archaeological findings about the stone circle. However, Stukeley was so carried away in his passion regarding the Celtic druids that his enthusiasm left its mark on almost all subsequent research.

A TEMPLE DEDICATED TO THE SUN

If one scientific fact has been affirmed during all of these centuries, it is the alignment of Stonehenge with the sunrise on the summer solstice. This fact has led researchers to consider as reliable the hypothesis that the monument was a temple dedicated to the sun

A Bluestone Altar

The outer circumference of Stonehenge, at 98 feet in diameter, is made up of vertical rectangular stones of sandstone crowned by lintels.

Inside this outer perimeter, another circle is found, made up of smaller pillars of bluestone, which encircle yet another structure in a horse-shoe shape, also built of sandstone rocks of the same color. Inside it is the mica sandstone slab known as the Slaughter Stone.

enigmas

What Was the Significance of the Bluestones?

One of the great mysteries which surrounds Stonehenge is that of the igneous blocks of rock (bluestones) with which the first circle of stones was made around 2500 BCE. The latest hypotheses claim that the Preseli Hills, and in particular the location of Carn Menyn, the exact source of the bluestone, were places of worship. Cuts in the rocks of the region have been found, dating back to the Neolithic period. In this sense, the second stage of Stonehenge would have artificially reproduced the great scenery of Carn Menyn.

To what end? Perhaps simply as a demonstration of the power of the local rulers – capable of bringing part of the sanctuary to their jurisdiction – or in order to transfer the supposed healing power of these stones to Stonehenge.

The belief that the natural springs of the Preseli Hills have medicinal qualities, widespread in the area until recent times, supports this hypothesis.

or an observatory establishing an annual calendar. Though the stones of Stonehenge continue hiding many mysteries, the archaeologists of the twenty-first century chose to distance themselves from the circle in order to gain perspective. The nearby remains of Woodhenge and Durrington Walls, as well as the sites where the stone blocks for the monument were extracted, have become the principal field of research in order to discover the function of Stonehenge.

A VAST CEMETERY

The new hypotheses combine the conclusions from the discoveries in these somewhat distant places with the analysis of the human remains buried around the monument. The dating of these remains demonstrate that Stonehenge had a definite burial purpose since its creation around the year 3000 BCE, until after the construction of the ring of silica sandstones, some 500 years later. According to Mike Parker Pearson, Professor of Archaeology at the University of Sheffield and co-director of the Stonehenge Riverside Project, the monument was erected in order to honor the ancestors. Drawing on his vast knowledge of the indigenous cultures of Madagascar, Parker Pearson arrived at the conclusion that the stones could symbolize the stiffening of the body after death as well as represent the everlastingness of eternal life; while the wooden constructions, made from more ephemeral material, could represent the brevity of earthly life. Though the high number of burials discovered – 240 total – make Stonehenge the largest Neolithic cemetery in England, the extensive period over which these ceremonies were celebrated makes one think that only the members of a royal family were buried at the monument, since only a few bodies were dug up from the first epoch and the number increased as the generations went by. This fact leads us to suppose that the neighboring henges of Durrington Walls and Woodhenge were considered the land of the living, in contrast to Stonehenge, the land of the dead.

CELEBRATION

For decades, thousands of people of diverse origins (hippies, druids – a title which denotes a religious class of Celts – new-agers, and other curious people) meet at sunrise at Stonehenge to celebrate the arrival of the northern summer in England. In recent years, up to 35,000 visitors have gathered, which has made the site ideal for tourism.

HOMAGE TO THE SUN

Many suppose that Stonehenge had this purpose, since its axis of prolongation along the great avenue is oriented toward the point where the sun rises on June 21 every year. Some specialists, such as the English astronomer Gerald Hawkings – whose theories were popular during the 60s – have claimed that it also predicts eclipses.

The Mysterious "Cursus"

The furrowed road, which is 2 miles long and 479 ft wide, was built 500 years before the first Stonehenge. Oriented toward the daybreak on the equinoxes in spring and autumn, it was called "cursus" by William Stukeley (image), who believed it was the remains of a chariot race stadium built by the Romans. More recent hypotheses speak of a processional avenue.

The fact that both places appear to be connected to the river by processional avenues, gives rise to the idea of a ceremonial circuit that represents the transition from life to death. According to Parker Pearson's hypothesis, the bodies of the members of the governing dynasty were taken from Durrington Walls to the river, and were taken down various miles by the current, on rafts made of tree trucks, to the avenue and on to Stonehenge, where they were buried after cremation. According to this idea, the remains of the commoner inhabitants of the region were not found because they were cremated and later thrown into the river as ashes. Other recent hypotheses consider Stonehenge to be a multi-functional center –cemetery, astronomical observatory, solar temple and healing sanctuary. This possibility would reconcile two of the irrefutable attributes of the monument: that it is filled with cremated human remains and that it is oriented toward the first sunrise of summer.

Durrington Walls Village

Archaeological studies show that the houses that made up the village are 4,600 years old. According to environmental analyses, it was a seasonal settlement housing people who traveled there with prepared foods and animals and only at certain times of the year.

A VILLAGE OF BUILDERS

According to studies done by the British archaeologist Mike Parker Pearson, in the Durrington Walls area there was an extensive circular village with more than 300 houses within it. With such dimensions, it was without a doubt one of the biggest villages in northwestern Europe. "We believe both men and women, and even children, lived there. And it would not have been unusual for all of them to have participated in the construction of the Stonehenge complex," states Parker Pearson.

Stone Age Remains

In one of the well-preserved houses found during the excavations funded by National Geographic, researchers discovered objects from daily life during the Stone Age: flint tools (axes, for example), the point of a brooch from a dress, and two niches the size of a teaspoon, in the corners of the house.

HOUSES OF CLAY, MORTAR, AND REEDS
After excavation work carried out in 2007, archaeologists found a series of houses with walls made of a mixture of ground clay and mortar (cobb) in some cases, and of reeds covered with mortar in others.

THE KITCHEN
In the center of the house, archaeologists found remnants of an oval stove and two gutters with ash stains around them. "Whoever cooked there was definitely kneeling," maintained Mike Parker Pearson.

The Tombs of Amesbury

A funerary site containing the remains of two men was discovered in Amesbury in 2002. The two men supposedly belong to the aristocracy of the period (one of them is the famous "Amesbury Archer"), and were accompanied by more than 100 objects, from arrowheads and copper knives to gold pendants.

Isotopic Analysis

This biochemical technology allows a broad range of information to be determined through the study of stable isotopes in archaeological remains: consumption of food resources, range of mobility, environmental characteristics, social hierarchy, and the populational, social, and economic dynamics pertaining to the civilization, among other things. Isotopes are variations of atoms of the same element. In nature, carbon is present in a mixture of three isotopes with mass numbers of 12, 13, and 14. Carbon-14 dating studies performed on archaeological pieces from Stonehenge some years ago at the Oxford University showed that the most likely date for the raising of the first stones was the year 2300 BCE.

KNIVES
Of copper, with well-sharpened points and of different sizes. Knives made of gold were also found.

BLACK STONE
Also called a "cushion stone" because of its similiarity to the cushions of a sofa, this stone was used as an anvil to work metal. Gold and copper were new to the men of the period in which Stonehenge was raised, and they had to seek out elements to work them.

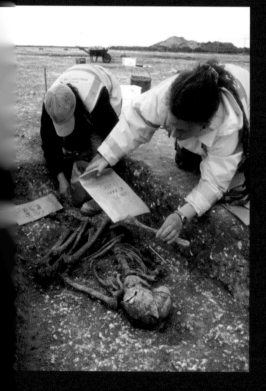

CARBON–14
During the excavation headed by British archaeologist Tim Darvill, 100 pieces of organic material from the bases of the original sandstone blocks were uncovered. 14 were

TUSK
It is thought that these belonged to a wild boar, or an animal of similar size, and that, during this time, they were used as

Prehistoric Migration

Analysis of the molars and premolars of the two adults found in the Amesbury tombs revealed that these people were in one place until six years of age and in another until age thirteen (possibly in the northwestern portion of Great Britain, Wales or Brittany). "This is the best example of prehistoric migration in Europe found to this day," stated British archaeologist Andrew Fitzpatrick.

EARRINGS
Made of gold, a material recently discovered at the time, they represent the earliest samples of jewelry work from the period. They were always found in pairs.

ARMBANDS
Used as protection during hunting, they also appeared to be a status symbol in the Celtic community. They were made of polished stone.

ORIGIN
Archaeologists claim that the "Amesbury Archer" came from the Alps near Switzerland and Germany.

ARROWHEADS
Fifteen of these arrowheads, of flint or silex (a very resistant mineral), were found near the body of the "Amesbury Archer."

OTHER TOMBS
A year after the discovery of the tomb of the archer and his companion, and less than half a mile away, other tombs from the same period containing the remains of seven people were found, four of them men.

Who Were Its Builders?

Until 4000 BCE, the tribes that populated Great Britain were nomadic and lived by hunting, gathering and fishing. Moving into the Neolithic period, they abandoned this simple subsistence life and began relying on agriculture and livestock.

When the construction of Stonehenge began, around 3000 BCE, the inhabitants of southwest England lived in very small groups, a circumstance that did not keep them from gathering in larger communities in order to complete more difficult tasks, such as, for example, the construction of a henge.

According to calculations, the third phase of construction on Stonehenge required two million hours of work, the equivalent of two years of labor for 300 men working ten hours a day. However, it is likely that the various clans in the region only dedicated part of the year to Stonehenge's construction, prolonging the task. The most recent research has calculated that in the settlement of Durrington Walls, near Stonehenge, there were 1,000 dwellings. Such size reinforces the hypotheses that this settlement was raised to house the monument's builders and the visitors arriving from various points in the region. In addition, analysis of the remains found seems to show that they did not spend the entire year there, but that they moved to the settlement, bringing what was needed to stay for a few months and help with the monument's construction.

NOMADISM AS THE NORM
Although they were largely stationary, Neolithic Britons also maintained nomadic habits to some extent. It was not unusual for them to spend part of the year away from their original locality. Every 10 to 20 years, they were essentially forced to leave the area where they lived and move in search of virgin ground to cultivate, as they did not yet know the agricultural techniques necessary to protect the soil's nutrients. This factor, combined with the destructive effects of ever-larger herds of cattle and goats, caused the region to lose a good part of its dense birch and pine forests in only a few centuries. As a result, by the time work began on Stonehenge, the meadows that we see today were already the dominant landscape.

What is still not completely understood is why Stonehenge became, in that time period, the region's great ritual center for a smaller than average people who wore skins, adorned themselves with animal teeth and bones, had an expected life span of some 35 years, and already practiced ancestor worship, this being one of the primary expressions of their spiritual beliefs.

The Case of the "Amesbury Archer"

In 2002, a group of archaeologists found two prehistoric tombs near Amesbury, a little more than 2 miles from Stonehenge. The remains, from around 2300 BCE, belonged to a man of about 40 years old and a younger relative, probably his son. The older man's tomb contained the best prehistoric funerary offerings found in Britain, including gold jewelry (the oldest remains of this type found on the islands), arrowheads, copper knives, and pieces of bell-shaped ceramic, a pottery technique commonly found throughout continental Europe, but not generally in Britain at this time. Analysis of dental remains turned up surprising information: the adult – dubbed the "Amesbury Archer" – was not a native of Britain, but of the Swiss Alps, and his young relative had been born locally.

It is thought that the archer emigrated from the continent and earned a prominent position in his new home thanks to his abilities, accumulating for himself great prestige and wealth.

Durrington Walls, a Camp for Workers?

Recent archaeological work at the Durrington Walls site, which contains two circles (northern and southern), and nearby Woodhenge, formed the basis of a convincing hypotheses regarding Stonehenge's purpose.

In 1812, a large henge was discovered near the small town of Durrington, 2 miles northeast of Stonehenge, in a bend of the Bristol River Avon. The circle was enormous, measuring 1500 feet in diameter, equivalent to twenty times the size of Stonehenge. Despite its proximity to the megalithic monument, the site was not excavated for the first time until 1966, and at the beginning of the twenty-first century it still kept nearly all of its secrets. Finally, in 2003, the henge of Durrington Walls, today crossed by a regional highway, became the central focus of the Stonehenge Riverside project, whose leaders discovered seven Neolithic dwellings to the east of the circle. These dwellings were built between 2600 and 2500 BCE, during the same period in which the bluestones were placed in Stonehenge. Researchers concluded that there may have been more than a thousand dwellings like those found, a figure that makes Durrington Walls the largest Neolithic settlement known in Great Britain. In one of the houses, researchers found a wall made of mortar using local limestone dust as its main ingredient. This material was used to cover the walls, which were constructed of a framework of thin branches and dung. Inside, archaeologists found signs of primitive wooden furniture and ceramic remnants, as well as animal bones, clear indications that the people of this area slept and ate here, at least during part of the year, suggesting it may have housed seasonal workforces.

VARIOUS RITUALS

Researchers also noted the scarcity of human remains, deducing that the population typically incinerated the bodies of their people and spread their ashes in the river. The remains of their leaders, however, appear to have been carried to Stonehenge in a ritual procession and interred near the great rock monument. There are three other smaller circular structures in the area, two inside the henge and the other, Woodhenge, located around 500 feet south of Durrington Walls. These three circles, of various diameters, show signs of wooden constructions. Discovered in 1925 during a plane flight, Woodhenge is situated near the large henge of Durrington Walls that was built around 2300 BCE. The remains of a wooden building were found in the interior of the embankment, and it was made up of six concentric rings of trunks supporting a thatched roof.

Seahenge: Preserved Wood

To understand the nature of henges with wood circles such as Woodhenge, archaeologists had to travel to a small coastal town in eastern England, Holme-next-the-Sea, near which, in 1998, the best-preserved prehistoric monument of this type was found: Seahenge, comprising of 55 trunks forming a circle some 23 feet in diameter, which was kept in good condition by the mud. In the center of the circle, the remains of an enormous inverted oak, with its roots for branches, was found. Through dendrochronology, it was established that the henge, whose magnificent state of preservation has been very useful in studying the morphology of these wooden monuments, was constructed in 2049 BCE, during the transition between the Neolithic period and the Bronze Age.

SEASONAL POPULATION
The broad circle of Durrington Walls, where dwellings of wood were built and inhabited by the builders of Stonehenge.

Stonehenge's Treasures

Since 2003, the Stonehenge Riverside Project, headed by Mike Parker Pearson of the University of Sheffield, has been discovering details about the life of the community that built the magnificent monument, thanks to the items found in various excavations in the area.

Dwelling Foundations

A decade ago, a group of archaeologists under Mike Parker Pearson found foundations for dwellings dating back 4,600 years, to the period in which construction on Stonehenge began. Excavations in the area surrounding the megalithic monument revealed the remains of eight wooden buildings, and study of the surrounding areas has revealed up to 30 more dwellings. A group of smaller dwellings was also found under the embankment. According to Parker Pearson, the cracks appearing in the plaster floor indicate that the local inhabitants cooked there. The remains of furnishings were also found in five of the dwellings. Test excavations and geophysical surveying have detected a multitude of additional possible chimneys in the valley. "I believe that we may find up to 300 dwellings at this site," Parker Pearson said during the excavation. If this is true, that makes it the largest Neolithic settlement found in Great Britain to date.

GNEISS STONE
This perforated and curiously polished stone is made of gneiss, a metamorphic rock composed of the same minerals found in granite (quartz, felds- par and mica), which was heavily used by the Britons who built Stonehenge. Today it is used to make stairs and pavers, and in masonry in general.

CONTAINER FOR BURNING INCENSE
Various groups (hippies, Masonic sects) meet at dawn on the summer solstice (June 21) to sing, spread oak leaves and burn incense in these containers, as it is believed the original inhabitants did during the era in which Stonehenge was constructed.

Horns and Bones of Livestock

According to studies by specialists, the workers who built Stonehenge, true engineering pioneers of the Bronze Age, managed to make holes in the ground with the precision their task demanded using solely meager digging tools made of the horns and bones of livestock. Archaeologists found these items buried in the deepest area of "the ditch," as it is referred to in English literature.

AXE
Made of silex, a material used frequently during the Stone Age, also known as flint. Its durability is ideal for making cutting tools such as the axes found at Stonehenge.

Arrowheads

Like the axes and other tools used by the Britons, the arrowheads found in the excavations performed recently were made of stone found in the Cornwall area, on the shores of the Celtic Sea. The British Isles, where the Stonehenge complex was built, were occupied by peoples from continental Europe whose men were migratory hunters. They used bows and arrows, like the Assyrians and Egyptians, and traveled in small wooden boats.

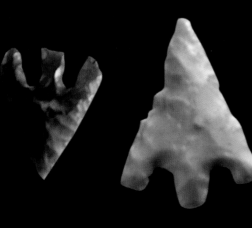

RING OF BRODGARD
This henge is part of the Heart of Neolithic Orkney, in the Orkney Islands. It forms part of a complex from the same era as Stonehenge.

Alternative Hypotheses

Was Stonehenge Connected to Other Megalithic Monuments?

This hypothesis assumes the existence of telluric energy lines that, when sensed by prehistoric peoples, allowed them to discern the ideal locations for holding ceremonies or placing sacred sites or temples. Alfred Watkins (1855–1935), an amateur archaeologist and prominent member of the Society for the Protection of Ancient Buildings in England, called these forces "ley lines," although they are also known as "energy lines" or "spiritual lines."

In 1925, Watkins described in his book *The Old Straight Track* how the primary megalithic constructions in England, including Stonehenge and many churches, were deliberately built on the remains of these energy centers. Watkins' works were revised, edited and popularized in 1960, and were perpetuated in *The View Over Atlantis* (1969) by researcher John Michell. Michell, who died in 2009, created the so-called "Michell line," based on the principles of Watkins' ley lines. The Michell line links to many dispersed sacred sites in England. The majority of these sites were Celtic in origin, and Christian churches were later erected over them. The direct correspondence between Stonehenge and Glastonbury, creating a connection with the ley lines related to other similar sites on the continents of Europe and Africa, stems from this.

REFUTATIONS
Today, the ideas of Alfred Watkins (photo), popular in the sixties, are not accepted by the majority of archaeologists.

Could It Be an Energy Generator?

This hypothesis arises from the idea of the "nemeton," a sacred place where the Celts held ceremonies to acquire life energy. But the most recent and reliable studies date the start of Stonehenge's construction as 5000 years ago; which is anachronous to this theory. Regardless, the ruins of that primitive site could have been used by the Celts for their rites, although in general, druids preferred forests or mountains to perform their particular ceremonies. Today, groups associated with druidic rites hold gatherings every solstice where hundreds of people hand in hand form a human chain around the monument. In this way, they claim, they are repeating today the rites performed by the Celts in their time to capture the fundamental energy present. They play harps and blow trumpets at dawn, burn incense, use mistletoe and oak leaves, and sing various prayers, with the idea of absorbing the energy, also considered curative, that supposedly emanates from the stones.

Is Stonehenge the Remains of a Roman Temple?

In the seventeenth century, the celebrated English architect Inigo Jones put forth that Stonehenge could have been a Roman temple. A protégé of King James I, Jones did not believe in the popular tales of Merlin the magician or in the fantastic epics told by Geoffrey of Monmouth. He believed instead that only a culture as developed as that of the Romans could have conceived a work like Stonehenge. He believed that he had discovered features associated with Tuscan columns on some monoliths, and drew up a detailed plan of the area, altering its geometry a little to conform it to the design of the circular Roman temples. In contrast, his opponents claimed that Stonehenge did not have traces of the reliefs and writing that usually adorned classic Roman buildings, and accused Jones of changing the drawing of the central horseshoe to a hexagon to make his theory fit. The architect died before he could respond to these criticisms, and his work was finally completed by a follower, John Webb.

What Was Merlin the Magician's Involvement?

The early writers of British history, such as Wace (1115–1170), Henry of Huntingdon (1080–1160), and particularly Geoffrey of Monmouth (1100–1155), alluded to Stonehenge as a sacred site. And it was Monmouth who added a touch of legend when he claimed that Merlin used his magic to move the stones from Ireland to Great Britain to build, under the commission of King Aurelius Ambrosius, a funerary monument for the great British rulers. In his writings, Monmouth confuses the name of this Celtic-Roman king, who, in reality, was called Ambrosius Aurelianus and lived in the fifth century. According to the legend, King Ambrosius sent Uther Pendragon (Arthur's father) to Ireland with 15,000 knights. The objective was to collect some magical rocks that had been carried there in the past by giants from the African continent. Monmouth did not indicate exactly where Pendragon went to search for the stones, but he precisely described the killing of 7,000 Irishmen commanded by Arthur's father to carry the valuable African stones to England. But the complications did not end there. When they attempted to move the stones using ropes, they failed dramatically. Then the magician Merlin intervened, deploying strange machinery complete with gears and other apparatus, along with other technical inventions, which allowed them to move the heavy cargo to England. Shortly thereafter, Ambrosius died, and his funeral christened the magnificent mausoleum. Uther Pendragon faced the same destiny. Arthur, on the other hand, was carried to the island of Avalon after his death. Other important monarchs from this legendary lineage rest at Stonehenge. Of course, this theory is completely fanciful and contradicts the latest carbon-14 measurements performed at the site.

BELIEF
Throughout the entire Middle Ages, Stonehenge was considered a physical testament to Merlin's magic.

What Role Did the Druids Play at Stonehenge?

English physician and archaeologist William Stukeley (1687–1765) was one of the first to suggest the hypothesis that Stonehenge had been constructed by the druids. He also speculated that the Phoenicians, who are believed to be ancestors of the Celts, had been the monument's builders. His hypotheses were built around his theory about religion: he believed that humanity, at its origins, had a fundamental patriarchal religion that, with the passing of time, had been subverted. Only the arrival of Jesus restored its original essence. Stukeley also considered Celtic Druidism a possible fundamental religion. After several years of study dedicated to Stonehenge, he considered it a defensible possibility that the megalithic monument had been constructed in 460 BCE by people arriving to the British Isles from the Near East. Some years before, John Aubrey (1626–1697) had come on the scene: a writer and student of antiquity dedicated specifically to the study of England's megalithic monuments, Aubrey suggested that Stonehenge was a temple built by the druids, an idea that some Masonic groups considered certain for many years.

PHOENICIANS
William Stukeley claimed that there were similarities between monuments from this civilization and Stonehenge.

Is Stonehenge a Representation of a Flying Saucer?

Tony Wedd, a Royal Air Force (RAF) pilot during the Second World War, who in time became a specialist in extraterrestrial life, has claimed that Stonehenge is the representation of a flying saucer, the result of the profound impression left on Neolithic Britons by the landing of a spaceship on Salisbury plains. According to Wedd, the ditch and embankment of the henge mark the edge of the saucer, and the Aubrey holes are its windows, like the openings on old ships that housed the cannons. The circle of siliceous sandstone emulates the cabin. Later, he went even further and was bold enough to conjecture that the neighboring cursus was the mother ship, larger and oblong in shape, that usually accompanies squadrons of flying saucers. The nearby population of Warminster, located to the west of Stonehenge, became famous during the sixties and seventies due to the number of UFO sightings there. Many specialists rule these out and attribute the confusion to RAF testing in the area.

Did Stonehenge Mimic the Halo Around the Sun and Moon?

Isaac N. Vail (1840–1912) was a Quaker philosopher and scientist from Ohio who defended an unusual hypothesis: in the millennia following the last ice age, the formation of a canopy or layer of ice crystals in the atmosphere was a phenomenon which would have created brilliant halos around the sun and moon. According to Vail, Stonehenge and other stone circles from Neolithic times were the representations created by the men of that time of these halos around the two largest astral bodies. In California, a magazine called *Stonehenge Viewpoint* has been published since the late seventies; its main objective is to spread Vail's ice canopy theory, as well as other information related to esoteric viewpoints of the monument. A series of books dedicated to this subject has also been published, in which archaeologists, astronomers, geologists and anthropologists discuss Vail's theory. Years later, Stonehenge specialist Donald L. Cyr defended Vail's theory in his book *Waters Above the Firmament* (1988).

Were the Hyperboreans the Builders of Stonehenge?

In his *Bibliotheca Historica,* consisting of 40 volumes divided into three sections, the Greek Diodorus Siculus (first century BCE) maintains that "on an island smaller than Sicily, located in the North Sea and called Hyperborea (a name given due to the profusion of Boreal winds in the area), there are magnificent enclosures dedicated to Apollo. And the grandest temple was spherical in shape and was always adorned with votive offerings."

Many historians and researchers consider that in this passage Diodorus is making reference to Great Britain, and, in particular, to Stonehenge. Diodorus also claims that the Hyperboreans, a civilization of gigantic immortal beings, came from the Iberian peninsula, where the first megalithic arrangements were found. A migration distributed them throughout various areas of Europe, including England, where they erected for the first time "a fantastic circle of stones," the monument today known as Stonehenge.

WHAT LEGEND SAYS
During the last interglacial period, the Hyperboreans abandoned the Arctic and moved to different areas of Europe, including the British Isles.

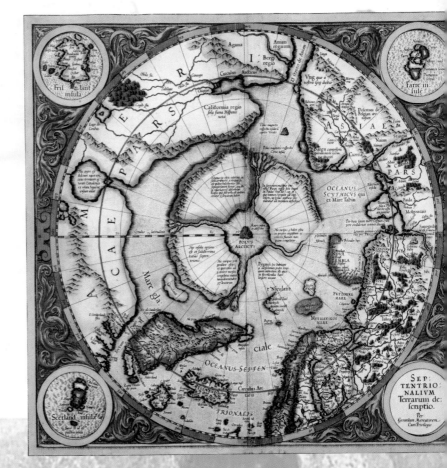

To See and Visit

▼ OTHER PLACES OF INTEREST

AVESBURY
GREAT BRITAIN

A few miles from Stonehenge, this picturesque and well-preserved town has a major attraction for those interested in archaeological treasures: the Avesbury Ring, a ring of stones that dates to the same period as Stonehenge, although they are much smaller.

BLUEHENGE
GREAT BRITAIN

Some years ago, a group of scientists discovered evidence of what they called "a second Stonehenge," with characteristics similar to the original. This archaeological site is located a little over 1 mile from the famous monument and was christened "Bluehenge" by specialists from the University of Sheffield due to the bluish appearance of the stones. Excavations show that a stone circle 30 feet in diameter was erected here, a complex that may have been surrounded by a ditch many years ago. It is also thought that the gigantic chunks of blue stone were brought from the Preseli Hills, more than 150 miles away.

SALISBURY CATHEDRAL
GREAT BRITAIN

In Wiltshire County, this impressive Anglican cathedral was begun in 1220 and finished a hundred years later. In 1790, important renovations were performed: the original choir loft was replaced, and the bell tower was demolished, which once stood 330 feet tall. An accurate example of English Gothic architecture, it is said that the cathedral possesses the oldest clock in the world (from 1386). It also

Stonehenge

MEGALITHIC MONUMENT

The British government has worked for years to promote tourism at Stonehenge. Visitors have at their disposal audio guides in nine languages, a variety of gastronomic offerings, and a special discount plan for group visits. Normal visiting hours are from 9 am to 7 pm, depending on weather conditions, which are generally unfavorable in winter.

DURRINGTON WALLS

The excavations performed at this site, 2 miles north of Stonehenge, indicate that it is the largest human settlement from the Neolithic period in Great Britain, eventually housing a community of several thousand inhabitants. It is surrounded by an enormous henge some 1500 feet in diameter, and despite the discovery of the remains of dwellings and utensils there, the majority of its secrets remain unknown.

THE AVENUE

This processional road that is approximately 75 feet wide and 2 miles long cuts through the ditch surrounding Stonehenge. Known as "The Avenue," this paved road aligns with the summer solstice, for which it is believed that it was used frequently during this time. The Avenue, discovered in the seventeenth century, connects Stonehenge to the River Avon.

Heel Stone

This stone, weighing 35 tons, whose tip coincides with the horizon, is just outside of and can be seen from Stonehenge. During the summer solstice (June 21), the sun peeks over the top of this stone, which has led to hypotheses about its astronomical function.

---

has an annex housing an outstanding octagonal chapter house with a large vault supported by a single central column. A must-see for tourists who find themselves near Wiltshire.

CARHENGE
UNITED STATES

Despite the fact that there is no relation between Stonehenge and the United States, there are numerous replicas of the monument here, some exact copies and others more or less inspired by the original. The tourist guide *Roadside America* published a list of the seven best imitations. The first replica was constructed by Sam Hill in Maryhill, Washington, paying homage to the soldiers killed in the First World War. The strangest is, without doubt, the one called Carhenge, built in

Alliance, Nebraska, using a series of automobiles painted grey.

THE HENGE
AUSTRALIA

Australia has its own Stonehenge replica. The originator of the project might seem unlikely: Ross Smith, an Australian brewer who proposed its construction as an additional attraction for those visiting the famous Margaret River wineries, located in southwest Australia. The structure, dubbed "The Henge," was built of 101 stones that, in total, amount to some 2,500 tons of granite mined in Esperance, a quarry located in the area near the wineries.

Glossary

AGRARIANISM A political or social philosophy that values rural society and farming over urban society.

ARABLE Suitable for farming.

CAMELID A mammal of the camel family, including llamas and alpacas.

CELESTIAL Relating to the sky or heavens.

CHIEFTAIN Leader of a group or clan.

CITADEL A fortress protecting a city.

CONCUBINE A woman who lives with a man but has a lower status than a wife.

CONQUEST The subjugation and control of a people or place by use of force.

DENDROCHRONOLOGY The scientific method of dating rings in a tree to the specific year they were formed to analyze atmospheric conditions during that time period.

DISINTERMENT Removal of human remains from a grave.

EMBANKMENT A wall of earth or stone built to prevent flooding.

ENDEMIC Native to a certain country or region.

ENIGMA Something that is mysterious or difficult to understand.

ENVOY A messenger or representative, usually on a diplomatic mission.

GARROTED Killed by strangulation.

HYDROLOGICAL Relating to water.

IDOLATRY Worship of images or representations of gods.

INCENDIARY Designed to cause fires.

MEGALITH A large stone that forms a prehistoric monument.

MORTAR A cuplike receptacle made of hard material.

NOMADIC Traveling from place to place with no permanent abode.

PINNACLE A high, pointed piece of rock.

POLYHEDRON A solid figure with many sides, usually more than six.

QUARRY A place from which stone is extracted, usually a pit.

SUBSISTENCE Maintaining or supporting oneself at a minimum level.

TELLURIC Of the earth or soil.

TRILITHON A structure made of two vertical stones with a third stone balanced horizontally on top of them.

TURRET A small tower on top of a larger tower or at the corner of a building or wall.

VICUÑA A member of the camel family that lives in the Andes.

Further Reading

Bauer, Brian S., and Charles Stanish. *Ritual and Pilgrimage in the Ancient Andes: The Islands of the Moon and Sun.* Austin, TX: University of Texas Press, 2001.

Castleden, Rodney. *The Stonehenge People: An Exploration of Life in Neolithic Britain, 4700-2000 B.C.* New York, NY: Routledge, 1990.

Fagen, Brian M., and Nadia Durrani. *People of the Earth: An Introduction to World Prehistory.* Fourteenth edition. New York, NY: Routledge, 2014.

Green, Jen. *Ancient Celts: Archaeology Unlocks the Secrets of the Celts' Past* (National Geographic Investigates). Washington, DC: National Geographic, 2008.

Lawson, Andrew J. *Chalkland: An Archaeology of Stonehenge and Its Region.* Salisbury, UK: Hobnob Press, 2007.

Murphy, John, ed. *Gods & Goddesses of the Inca, Maya, and Aztec Civilizations* (Gods and Goddesses of Mythology). New York, NY: Britannica Educational Publishing with Rosen Educational Services, 2015.

Quilter, Jeffrey. *The Civilization of the Incas* (The Illustrated History of the Ancient World). New York, NY: Rosen Educational Publishing, 2013.

Reinhard, Johann. *Machu Picchu: Exploring an Ancient Sacred Center.* Los Angeles, CA: Cotsen Institute of Archaeology (UCLA), 2007.

Southern, Patricia. *The Story of Stonehenge.* Gloucestershire, UK: Amberley Publishing, 2014.

Websites

Historic Sanctuary of Machu Picchu

http://whc.unesco.org/en/list/274

UNESCO provides information for visitors to Machu Picchu—including maps—along with galleries of photos and videos of the site.

Ice Mummies of the Inca

http://www.pbs.org/wgbh/nova/ancient/ice-mummies-inca.html

This page from PBS details the discovery and excavation of Incan ice mummies, including Juanita. The website also goes into the history of the mummies and includes images from the excavation.

Stonehenge— English Heritage

http://www.english-heritage.org.uk/visit/places/stonehenge/

This website from the English Heritage Organization features information on the history of Stonehenge, a virtual tour, and useful information for visitors.

Index